AS/A... ...9

Series Editor: Ma...

Emily Brontë

Philip Allan Updates
Market Place
Deddington
Oxfordshire
OX15 0SE
Tel: 01869 338652
Fax: 01869 337590
e-mail: sales@philipallan.co.uk
www.philipallan.co.uk

Printed by Raithby, Lawrence & Co Ltd, Leicester

Environmental information
The paper on which this title is printed is sourced from managed, sustainable forests.

Contents

Introduction

Aims of the guide

The purpose of this Student Text Guide to Emily Brontë's *Wuthering Heights* is to enable you to organise your thoughts and responses to the novel, to deepen your understanding of key feature and aspects, and finally to help you to address the particular requirements of examination questions in order to obtain the best possible grade. It will also prove useful to those writing a coursework piece on the novel by providing a number of summaries, lists, analyses and references to help with the content and construction of the assignment. Page references throughout are to the 2003 Penguin edition of the text.

It is assumed that you have read and studied the novel already under the guidance of a teacher or lecturer. This is a revision guide, not an introduction, although some of its content serves the purpose of providing initial background. It can be read in its entirety in one sitting, or it can be dipped into and used as a reference guide to specific and separate aspects of the novel.

The remainder of this Introduction section consists of exam board specifications and Assessment Objectives, which summarise in detail the requirements of the various boards and their schemes of assessment, a revision scheme which gives a suggested programme for using the material in the guide and advice on writing examination essays.

The Text Guidance section examines key aspects of the book including contexts, sources and interpretations.

The final section, Questions and Answers, includes mark schemes, model essay plans and some examples of marked work.

Assessment Objectives

These are set by QCA and are common to all boards. Those relevant to this text are:

AO1	communicate clearly the knowledge, understanding and insight appropriate to literary study, using appropriate terminology and accurate and coherent written expression
AO2i	respond with knowledge and understanding to literary texts of different types and periods
AO2ii	respond with knowledge and understanding to literary texts of different types and periods, exploring and commenting on relationships and comparisons between literary texts

AO3	show detailed understanding of the ways in which writers' choices of form, structure and language shape meanings
AO4	articulate independent opinions and judgements, informed by different interpretations of literary texts by other readers
AO5i	show understanding of the contexts in which literary texts are written and understood
AO5ii	evaluate the significance of cultural, historical and other contextual influences on literary texts and study

This can be summarised as:

AO1	clarity of written communication
AO2	informed personal response in relation to time and genre (literary context)
AO3	the creative literary process (context of writing)
AO4	critical and interpretative response (context of reading)
AO5	evaluation of influences (cultural context)

Wuthering Heights has a total weighting of 30%, divided as follows:

Edexcel	Unit 6: AO1 – 5%; AO2ii – 15%; AO3 – 10%; AO4 – 5%; AO5ii – 5%
OCR	Unit 2708: AO1 – 10%; AO2i – 10%; AO3 – 10%; AO4 – 5%; AO5i – 5%
AQA (B)	Module 1: AO1 – 10%; AO2i – 5%; AO3 – 10%; AO4 – 5%; AO5i – 5%

Note the significantly different weighting of the Assessment Objectives between the different examining boards for the same text. It is essential that you pay close attention to the AOs, and their weighting, for the board for which you are entered. These are what the examiner will be looking for, and you must address them *directly* and *specifically*, in addition to proving general familiarity with and understanding of the text, and being able to present an argument clearly, relevantly and convincingly.

Note that the examiners are seeking above all else evidence of an *informed personal response* to the text. A revision guide such as this can help you to understand the text and to form your own opinions, but it cannot replace your own ideas and responses as an individual reader.

Revision advice

For the examined units it is possible that either brief or more extensive revision will be necessary because the original study of the text took place some time previously. It is therefore useful to know how to go about revising and which tried and tested methods are considered the most successful for literature exams at all levels, from GCSE to degree finals. Below is a guide on how not to do it — think of reasons why not in each case.

Don't:

- leave it until the last minute
- assume you remember the text well enough and don't need to revise at all
- spend hours designing a beautiful revision schedule
- revise more than one text at the same time
- think you don't need to revise because it is an open book exam
- decide in advance what you think the questions will be and revise only for those
- try to memorise particular essay plans
- reread texts randomly and aimlessly
- revise for longer than 2 hours in one sitting
- miss school lessons in order to work alone at home
- try to learn a whole ring-binder's worth of work
- tell yourself that character and plot revision is enough
- imagine that watching the video again is the best way to revise
- rely on a study guide instead of the text

There are no short-cuts to effective exam revision; the only way to know a text extremely well, and to know your way around it in an exam, is to have done the necessary studying. If you use the following method, in six easy stages, for both open and closed book revision, you will not only revisit and reassess all your previous work on the text in a manageable way but will be able to distil, organise and retain your knowledge. Don't try to do it all in one go: take regular breaks for refreshment and a change of scene.

(1) Between a month and a fortnight before the exam, depending on your schedule (a simple list of stages with dates displayed in your room, not a work of art!), you will need to reread the text, this time taking stock of all the underlinings and marginal annotations as well. As you read, collect onto sheets of A4 the essential ideas and quotations as you come across them. The acts of selecting key material and recording it as notes are natural ways of stimulating thought and aiding memory.

(2) Reread the highlighted areas and marginal annotations in your critical extracts and background handouts, and add anything useful from them to your list of notes and quotations. Then reread your previous essays and the teacher's comments. As

you look back through essays written earlier in the course, you should have the pleasant sensation of realising that you can now write much better on the text than you could then. You will also discover that much of your huge file of notes is redundant or repeated, and that you have changed your mind about some beliefs, so that the distillation process is not too daunting. Selecting what is important is the way to crystallise your knowledge and understanding.

(3) During the run-up to the exam you need to do lots of practice essay plans to help you identify any gaps in your knowledge and give you practice in planning in 5–8 minutes. Past paper titles for you to plan are provided in this guide, some of which can be done as full timed essays — and marked strictly according to exam criteria — which will show whether length and timing are problematic for you. If you have not seen a copy of a real exam paper before you take your first module, ask to see a past paper so that you are familiar with the layout and rubric.

(4) About a week before the exam, reduce your two or three sides of A4 notes to a double-sided postcard of very small, dense writing. Collect a group of keywords by once again selecting and condensing, and use abbreviations for quotations (first and last word), and character and place names (initials). (For the comparison unit your postcard will need to refer to key points, themes and quotations in both texts relevant to the specific theme or genre topic.) The act of choosing and writing out the short quotations will help you to focus on the essential issues, and to recall them quickly in the exam. Make sure that your selection covers the main themes and includes examples of symbolism, style, comments on character, examples of irony, point of view or other significant aspects of the text. Previous class discussion and essay writing will have indicated which quotations are useful for almost any title; pick those which can serve more than one purpose, for instance those which reveal character and theme, and are also an example of language. In this way a minimum number of quotations can have maximum application.

(5) You now have in a compact, accessible form all the material for any possible essay title. There are only half a dozen themes relevant to a literary text so if you have covered these, you should not meet with any nasty surprises when you read the exam questions. You do not need to refer to your file of paperwork again, or even to the text. For the few days before the exam, you can read through your handy postcard whenever and wherever you get the opportunity. Each time you read it, which will only take a few minutes, you are reminding yourself of all the information you will be able to recall in the exam to adapt to the general title or to support an analysis of particular passages.

(6) A fresh, active mind works wonders, and information needs time to settle, so don't try to cram just before the exam. Relax the night before and get a good night's sleep. Then you will be able to enter the exam room with all the confidence of a well-prepared candidate.

Writing examination essays

Essay content

One of the key skills you are being asked to demonstrate at A-level is the ability to select and tailor your knowledge of the text and its background to the question set in the exam paper. In order to reach the highest levels, you need to avoid 'pre-packaged' essays which lack focus, relevance and coherence, and which simply contain everything you know about the text. Be ruthless in rejecting irrelevant material, after considering whether it can be made relevant by a change of emphasis. Aim to cover the whole question, not just part of it; your response needs to demonstrate breadth and depth, covering the full range of text elements: character, event, theme and language. Only half a dozen approaches are possible for any set text, though they may be phrased in a variety of ways, and they are likely to refer to the key themes of the text. Preparation of the text therefore involves extensive discussion and practice at manipulating these core themes so that there should be no surprises in the exam. An apparently new angle is more likely to be something familiar presented in an unfamiliar way and you should not panic or reject the choice of question because you think you know nothing about it.

Exam titles are open-ended in the sense that there is not an obvious right answer, and you would therefore be unwise to give a dismissive, extreme or entirely one-sided response. The question would not have been set if the answer were not debatable. An ability and willingness to see both sides is an Assessment Objective and shows independence of judgement as a reader. Do not be afraid to explore the issues and do not try to tie the text into one neat interpretation. If there is ambiguity it is likely to be deliberate on the part of the author and must be discussed; literary texts are complex and often paradoxical, and it would be a misreading of them to suggest that there is only one possible interpretation. You are not expected, however, to argue equally strongly or extensively for both sides of an argument, since personal opinion is an important factor. It is advisable to deal with the alternative view at the beginning of your response, and then construct your own view as the main part of the essay. This makes it less likely that you will appear to cancel out your own line of argument.

Choosing the right question

The first skill you must show when presented with the exam paper is the ability to choose the better, for you, of the two questions on your text where there is a choice. This is not to say you should always go for the same type of essay (whole-text or passage-based) and if the question is not one which you feel happy with for any reason, you should seriously consider the other, even if it is not the type you normally prefer. It is unlikely but possible that a question contains a word you are not sure you know the meaning of, in which case it would be safer to choose the other one.

Do not be tempted to choose a question because of its similarity to one you have already done. Freshness and thinking on the spot usually produce a better result than attempted recall of a previous essay which may have received only a mediocre mark in the first place. The exam question is unlikely to have exactly the same focus and your response may seem 'off centre' as a result, as well as stale and perfunctory in expression. Essay questions fall into the following categories: close section analysis and relation to whole text; characterisation; setting and atmosphere; structure and effectiveness; genre; language and style; themes and issues. Remember, however, that themes are relevant to all essays and that analysis, not just description, is always required.

Once you have decided which exam question to attempt, follow the procedure below for whole-text and passage-based, open- and closed-book essays.

(1) Underline all the key words in the question and note how many parts the question has.

(2) Plan your answer, using aspects of the key words and parts of the question as sub-headings, in addition to themes. Aim for 10–12 ideas. Check that the Assessment Objectives are covered.

(3) Support your argument by selecting the best examples of characters, events, imagery and quotations to prove your points. Remove ideas for which you can find no evidence.

(4) Structure your answer by grouping and numbering your points in a logical progression. Identify the best general point to keep for the conclusion.

(5) Introduce your essay with a short paragraph setting the context and defining the key words in the question as broadly, but relevantly, as possible.

(6) Write the rest of the essay, following your structured plan but adding extra material if it occurs to you. Paragraph your writing and consider expression, especially sentence structure and vocabulary choices, as you write. Signal changes in the direction of your argument with paragraph openers such as 'Furthermore' and 'However'. Use plenty of short, integrated quotations and use the words of the text rather than your own where possible. Use technical terms appropriately, and write concisely and precisely, avoiding vagueness and ambiguity.

(7) Your conclusion should sound conclusive and make it clear that you have answered the question. It should be an overview of the question and the text, not a repetition or a summary of points already made.

(8) Cross out your plan with a neat diagonal line.

(9) Check your essay for content, style, clarity and accuracy. With neat crossings-out, correct errors of fact, spelling, grammar and punctuation. Improve expression if possible, and remove any repetition and irrelevance. Add clarification and missing evidence, if necessary, using omission marks or asterisks. Even at this stage, good new material can be added.

There is no such thing as a perfect or model essay; flawed essays can gain full marks. There is always something more which could have been said, and examiners realise that students have limitations when writing under pressure in timed conditions. You are not penalised for what you didn't say in comparison to some idealised concept of the answer, but rewarded for the knowledge and understanding you have shown. It is not as difficult as you may think to do well, provided that you are familiar with the text and have sufficient essay-writing experience. If you follow the above process and **underline**, **plan**, **support**, **structure**, **write** and **check**, you can't go far wrong.

Text Guidance

Contexts

Historical context

About Emily Brontë

1818	30 July, born at Thornton, near Bradford, Yorkshire.
1820	April, the Brontë family moves to Haworth.
1821	September, mother dies.
1824	November, attends Cowan Bridge School.
1825	Two older sisters die; Charlotte and Emily leave Cowan Bridge.
1831	Emily and Anne begin their imaginary Gondal saga.
1834	Earliest dated Emily Brontë manuscript.
1836	Earliest dated poem.
1837	Teaches at Law Hill School; remains there about 6 months.
1838–42	Over half of Emily's surviving poems written.
1842	Spends 10 months at school in Brussels with Charlotte; returns to Haworth after the death of Aunt Branwell.
1845	Charlotte and Emily collaborate on a volume of poems; begins *Wuthering Heights*.
1846	Poems by Currer, Ellis and Acton Bell published; *Wuthering Heights* completed.
1847	*Wuthering Heights* and *Agnes Grey* published.
1848	September, Branwell dies; Emily leaves home for the last time to attend his funeral; 19 December, Emily dies.
1850	*Wuthering Heights* reissued, with a selection of poems and a biographical notice by Charlotte.
1941	Hatfield's edition of *The Complete Poems of Emily Jane Brontë* published.

Biographical sketch

Emily Brontë was the fifth child of the Reverend Patrick Brontë, a stern evangelical curate, and his wife Maria. After her mother died of cancer when she was only 3 years old, Emily and her five siblings were brought up by their father and their Aunt Branwell, a strict Calvinist, who moved in to help the family. They lived in a parsonage in Haworth with the bleak moors of Yorkshire on one side and the parish graveyard on the other.

From the age of 6, Emily attended a boarding school, where her sisters were already enrolled. The school was run with the intention of punishing the pupils' bodies in order that their souls might be saved. The students were hungry, cold, tired, and often ill. After the deaths of their older sisters from tuberculosis, Charlotte and Emily returned to Haworth, where they spent the rest of their childhood with their father, their sister Anne and their notoriously wild and mysterious brother, Branwell, isolated on the beautiful but inhospitable moors.

Emily rarely spent any time away from home. In 1835, at the age of 17, she went to Roe Head, where Charlotte was teaching, but became so ill that her sister was convinced she would die unless she returned home. She left home in 1837 and in 1842, on the latter occasion to study in Belgium, but both times was unable to bear a long separation from her beloved, wild homeland. She could not adapt to the demands of living the life of a genteel Victorian lady, nor could she ever fit in fully with strangers. She never made any close friends outside her family circle.

About the novel

First published in 1847, under the nom de plume of Ellis Bell, *Wuthering Heights* is Emily Brontë's only novel. Perhaps not surprisingly, given its immense brutality and thinly veiled sexual passion, it shocked and affronted many of its earliest readers, although it did enjoy modest success. It gained greater renown after 1848, owing to Emily's death, the increasing popularity of the novels of Charlotte and Anne Brontë, and public fascination with the immense concentration of talent in the Brontë family. Interest in and speculation about the biographical details of their lives, the sisters' relationships with their infamous brother Branwell, and the links between these and their fiction has hardly declined, and *Wuthering Heights* remains an astonishing work of passion and wildness. Like other great novels such as *Frankenstein* and *Dracula*, it has become part of the very blood of both literary and popular culture. Unlike other novels of its time, such as those of Charles Dickens, Elizabeth Gaskell, Benjamin Disraeli, Wilkie Collins and Charles Kingsley, *Wuthering Heights* does not really engage with the great social issues of the day, although these do impinge on the world of the novel; instead, it seems to link more readily with the world of Gothic fiction and the Romantics.

Gothic context

Typical aspects of the Gothic

While many critics have seen the Gothic as a loosely defined form, it is nevertheless possible to identify a wide range of features typical of works that fall within the genre. The following list covers the most common, all of which are highly significant in a consideration of *Wuthering Heights*:

- **wild landscapes** — the brooding yet strikingly beautiful moors and Penistone Crags; also the dark and threatening streets of Liverpool from which Heathcliff is rescued

- **ruined or grotesque buildings** — typically castles, granges, houses, mansions; in *Wuthering Heights* the role is fulfilled by the Grange, in its isolation and starkness, but more explicitly by the Heights, a place of brutal exposure and glowering threat
- **religious settings/religious concepts** — churches, abbeys, monasteries, convents
- **sensibility** — the cult of emotion, sudden shifts of emotion
- **excess and extremity** — extremes of location, emotion, violence, cruelty and perversion abound in *Wuthering Heights*
- **the supernatural and ghostly** — Cathy and Heathcliff both fulfil this role, during life and after death; figurative 'ghosts' of the past or the future which haunt the characters
- **imagery of darkness, shadow, decay** — the moor, the Heights, Linton, Heathcliff, Cathy and the churchyard are all vehicles of darkness, shadow and decay
- **the exotic and oriental** — the uncertain racial background of Heathcliff is significant, as is the general distrust of 'foreigners' expressed by the characters; in the claustrophobic world of the novel, however, the foreign often exists near to hand
- **horror and terror**
- **isolation and loneliness** — this relates to both setting and character, including orphaning and widowing
- **blurring of distinctions between sanity and insanity**
- **sex and sexuality** — includes obvious sexual overtones of the frequently used towers (phallus) and caverns (vagina)
- **use of multiple narrators**
- **crime, lawlessness and abuse**
- **absolute power** — often tyrannical and including abuse
- **stock characters** — absent mother, wicked father/father-figure, helpless heroine, the villain (often linked to religion), hopeless lover, criminal
- **the devilish and arcane**
- **use of the historical past** — interestingly absent from *Wuthering Heights*, which is given a contemporary setting, although the novel depends entirely on the presentation of the 'histories' of the central characters
- **the outsider**

Brontë employs these devices extensively, yet *Wuthering Heights* cannot be seen as conventionally Gothic in the sense that the works of Ann Radcliffe or Matthew Lewis are, as any comparison with these authors will make clear. However, Brontë relies to a significant extent upon the stock tools of the Gothic genre. You need to be prepared and able to consider the use and subversion of Gothic convention within the novel.

Roots and manifestations of the Gothic

The Gothic first emerged as a recognisable form in the mid- to late-eighteenth century. *The Recess* (Sophia Lee), *The Old English Baron* (Clara Reeve) and *The Castle of Otranto* (Horace Walpole) all date from this period and are generally recognised as the first flourishing of the form. It was with the works of Ann Radcliffe (*The Mysteries of Udolpho, The Romance of the Forest* and *The Italian*) and Matthew 'Monk' Lewis (*The Monk*) that the classic nature of the form and a fuller critical definition of it began to be established. These two authors may be taken to represent the two contradictory impulses in the Gothic between the literature of terror and the literature of horror. The genre continued to develop in the work of authors such as Charles Maturin (*Melmoth the Wanderer*), James Hogg (*The Private Memoirs and Confessions of a Justified Sinner*), William Godwin (*Caleb Williams*) and his daughter Mary Shelley, whose greatest novel is *Frankenstein*.

In the Victorian era, Gothic continued to develop in the work of Sheridan le Fanu (*Uncle Silas, The Wyvern Mystery*) and in the tales of Elizabeth Gaskell, among others. A new direction was established, however, through the sensation novels of authors such as Wilkie Collins and Mary Elizabeth Braddon. Towards the end of the nineteenth century and into the twentieth, new versions of the form continued to proliferate in the decadence of Oscar Wilde (*The Picture of Dorian Gray*), Robert Louis Stevenson (*Dr Jekyll and Mr Hyde*) and Bram Stoker (*Dracula*), the ghost stories of Henry James, M. R. James and Sir Arthur Conan Doyle, and the great adventure novels of Doyle, H. Rider Haggard and H. G. Wells. In all of these writers, where fear of the outsider in the closing years of empire is paramount, the way is paved for the more overtly arcane and horrific that has tended to dominate the form over the last century.

Roots of the Gothic

The roots of the Gothic precede the works of Walpole, Lee and Reeve. The following list suggests a number of the key authors and movements that influenced the rise of the Gothic form:

- **Elizabethan and Jacobean tragedy** — supernatural, vice, corruption, imprisonment, brutality, sexuality
- **graveyard poetry** — Blair, Young, Parnell; focus on decay and death
- **William Blake** — the dimension of the religious; the essential coexistence of opposites
- **the Romantics** — notably Wordsworth, Coleridge and de Quincey; focus on the natural world and its relation to the state of mankind
- **the novel of sensibility** — excess of emotion and extremity
- **Milton** — the dimension of religion; the battle between good and evil
- **medieval Gothic** — the focus on the grotesque, gargoyles

Manifestations of the Gothic

There are inevitable difficulties in attempting to define any genre. This difficulty is multiplied in relation to the Gothic, because the form has taken on many different manifestations. In addition, there are many sub-groups, such as some branches of science fiction, the Western, the thriller and the detective novel, which frequently make use of the techniques of Gothic while never fully engaging with it. Below is a broad outline of the various mainstream forms.

- romance (Ann Radcliffe, Charlotte Dacre, Clara Reeve)
- sensation (Wilkie Collins, Mary Elizabeth Braddon)
- mystery/adventure (Sir Arthur Conan Doyle, H. Rider Haggard, H. G. Wells)
- fantasy (H. G. Wells, J. R. R. Tolkien, Mervyn Peake)
- ghost story (Henry James, M. R. James, Sir Arthur Conan Doyle, Susan Hill)
- horror (Edgar Allan Poe, James Herbert, Stephen King)
- arcane (H. P. Lovecraft)
- decadence (Robert Louis Stevenson, Oscar Wilde, H. G. Wells, Bram Stoker, Arthur Machen)

The reading list at the end of this guide provides plentiful additional and comparative reading material, enabling you to undertake a structured course of private reading to extend your response to the novel through comparison with a range of other texts. This will help to develop your awareness of the typical elements of the Gothic form in its various manifestations, and to consider how they inform one another.

Dualisms within the Gothic

The Gothic is a form that thrives on the fruitful recognition of opposition and division. As critics have observed repeatedly, it is a genre that abides on the borders and extremes of experience, and as such the stark use of opposition is both appropriate and unavoidable. The very nature of the genre depends upon uncertainty and the possibility of violent shifts. The unsettling and the indefinable have a central role to play in any Gothic novel, and *Wuthering Heights* is no exception. If we are to be disturbed and unsure about the true nature of what we see, the deployment of uncertainty through opposites is essential. The concept of uncertainty is of particular importance in *Wuthering Heights*, as the novel deals with questions of moral, social, religious and personal doubt. Brontë presents a world where distinctions are blurred and where confusion is prevalent over action, motive, emotion and even individuality. This is true not only of *Wuthering Heights*, but of Gothic fiction, poetry and drama in general, where the recognition of opposition and uncertainty is one of the key areas of concern. The appearance of these issues within the Gothic genre is frequently allied to political and social concerns, and is often reflected in periods of social, religious and moral unrest.

Below is a list of a number of the most commonly used oppositions and divisions within the genre:

- good/evil
- innocence/guilt
- Catholic/Protestant
- freedom/imprisonment
- pursued/pursuer
- natural/unnatural
- terror/horror
- moral/immoral/amoral
- light/dark

- male/female
- reality/fantasy
- natural/supernatural
- human/inhuman
- internal/external
- high/low (mountains/abysses)
- small/large
- the defined/the undefined
- living/dead/undead

The impact of such oppositions and their use in the Gothic novel is profoundly unsettling for the reader. This is certainly significant in considering the author's intentions. The inhabitants of the Grange and the Heights face a sequence of momentous social, religious, ethical and personal choices, all of which may be summed up in pairs of opposites. Brontë's presentation of these issues is never straightforward, and the reader's response cannot be straightforward either. The ambiguity we feel in relation to the central issues of the novel leads to a deep ambivalence in our attitude towards the characters and scenarios portrayed. Such a response encapsulates the essentially contradictory nature of the Gothic genre.

Gothic images

Many artists have worked in what may be termed a Gothic style. William Blake and Goya are two of the best known examples, alongside the French artist, Gustave Doré. Blake was both a poet and an artist, producing a sequence of books which were a synthesis of pictures and words; he considered that the two were inseparable in his art, and as such an informed 'reading' of his pictures is essential to an understanding of his work. A number of his works adopt the typical Gothic device of working through opposites, such as *The Songs of Innocence and Experience* and *The Marriage of Heaven and Hell*. He also produced images for such evocatively named poems as 'The Grave' by Robert Blair and 'The Complaint, or, Night-thoughts on Life, Death and Immortality' by Edward Young. Goya is another highly significant figure, referred to by Richard Davenport-Hines (1998) as 'the greatest painter to have had gothic moods'. Goya also recognised this propensity in himself when he wrote: 'Fantasy abandoned by reason produces impossible monsters.'

In approaching a Gothic text such as *Wuthering Heights*, it is essential to be aware of not only the literary but also the artistic context of writing. You will find an exploration of some examples of Gothic art both an enlightening and a fascinating exercise. Emily Brontë, along with other great authors of Gothic, such as Edgar Allan Poe, Charles Maturin, Ann Radcliffe and Matthew 'Monk' Lewis, depends to a great extent on the visual impact of her words. As you read, take time to visualise the scenes she paints for you.

Try to spend some time looking at some or all of the following pictures, all of which are available on the internet:

- **Goya** — *The Sleep of Reason Produces Monsters* (*El Sueño de la Razon Produce Monstruos*). Davenport-Hines refers to this painting as 'Perhaps the most important single image for the historian of the gothic'.
- **William Blake** — *Good and Evil Angels*
- **Henry Fuseli** — *The Nightmare*
- **Caspar David Friedrich** — *The Cross in the Mountains*

When you look at these paintings, try to identify the typical themes and concerns of the Gothic which are identified earlier in this book. Look closely at a range of these images and use them as the basis of a series of short reflections, outlining the ways in which these paintings can illuminate our understanding of the Gothic form. Pay particular attention to the Goya painting, which is reproduced here.

*The Sleep of Reason
Produces Monsters
(El Sueño de la Razon
Produce Monstruos)*

Literary contexts

Brontë's poems

Emily Brontë wrote only one novel. However, she did write a significant number of poems, many of which reflect thematically and linguistically upon *Wuthering Heights*. Below is a sequence of four extracts from her Collected Poems, each of which offers the student an interesting set of parallels to the novel.

> Sleep brings no joy to me
> Remembrance never dies
> My soul is given to misery
> And lives in sighs
>
> Sleep brings no rest to me
> The shadows of the dead
> My waking eyes may never see
> Surround my bed
>
> Sleep brings no hope to me
> In soundest sleep they come
> And with their doleful imagery
> Deepen the gloom
>
> Sleep brings no wish to knit
> My harassed heart beneath
> My only wish is to forget
> In the sleep of death
>
> (*The Complete Poems*, p. 55)

*   *   *

> Cold in the earth — and the deep snow piled above thee,
> Far, far, removed, cold in the dreary grave!
> Have I forgot, my only Love, to love thee,
> Severed at last by Time's all-severing wave?
>
> (*The Complete Poems*, p. 8)

*   *   *

> Glad comforter! Will I not brave,
> Unawed, the darkness of the grave?
> Nay, smile to hear Death's billows rave —
> Sustained, my guide, by thee?

The more unjust seems present fate,
The more my spirit swells elate,
Strong, in thy strength, to anticipate
Rewarding destiny!

(The Complete Poems, p. 12)

*   *   *

So, if a tear, when thou art dying,
Should haply fall from me,
It is but that my soul is sighing,
To go and rest with thee.

(The Complete Poems, p. 29)

In these poems Brontë makes use of various easily identified elements from the Gothic tradition, all of which are shared with the fictional world of *Wuthering Heights*. There are numerous images of:

■ death	■ sleeplessness	■ graveyards
■ storm	■ sadness	■ hopelessness
■ coldness	■ desperation	■ gloom
■ separation	■ isolation	■ darkness

Note too the heavy emphasis placed on the spirit and the spiritual within the poems. This relates clearly to the world of Gothic fiction, where the spiritual and the ghostly worlds come to the fore so frequently. Accompanying all of these issues is Brontë's use of excess of emotion; this connects both to the Romantic roots of much of Brontë's work and to the prevalence of the sentimental novel in the development of the Gothic genre.

Links between Brontë's poems and *Wuthering Heights*

As well as possessing generic similarities to the world of the Gothic in general, these poems provide a number of significant parallels to *Wuthering Heights*. In particular, there are a number of specific links to the relationship between Heathcliff and Cathy:

- **untimely separation by death** — both Heathcliff and Cathy are aware of what they lose in the separation imposed by Cathy's early death
- **extreme and lasting response to death** — Heathcliff is tormented for 18 years by his unfulfilled union with Cathy
- **overpowering sense of spiritual connection** — Heathcliff and Cathy are so close as to seem almost subsumed within one another at times
- **inability to sleep** — Heathcliff does much walking alone at nights, as does Cathy's ghost

- **removal of a loved one to the grave** — Cathy is removed from Heathcliff to the grave, and the novel explores, as the poems suggest, the question of whether such links can ever be severed
- **significance of the grave** — this is explored in detail in the novel
- **dreariness and crumbling decay of the churchyard** — this carries great symbolic weight in the novel, both as a Gothic device and in terms of the novel's presentation of religious views and the role of the human spirit
- **death envisaged as a storm** — this idea is pertinent when applied to the deaths of Cathy and Heathcliff, as neither gains either peace or rest from death
- **the departed as a spiritual 'guide'** — Heathcliff is sustained and tormented by his 'guide', Cathy, through the rest of his life
- **mutual interdependence** — Heathcliff and Cathy are unable to find happiness without each other
- **desire for death** — Cathy longs for the death that will separate her from Edgar and that will be a living torment to Heathcliff; Heathcliff yearns for the death that will reconcile him with himself and reunite him with Cathy. This concept supports a Freudian reading of the novel.

Wuthering Heights and King Lear

The comparison of Brontë's novel with Shakespeare's tragedy is invoked initially by Brontë herself. Early in the novel and against his will, like the hapless King Lear in his daughter's house, Lockwood finds himself imprisoned and maltreated by the servants of the household at Wuthering Heights. This is a parallel which Lockwood draws explicitly himself (p. 17):

> …then, hatless and trembling with wrath, I ordered the miscreants to let me out — on their peril to keep me one minute longer — with several incoherent threats of retaliation that, in their indefinite depth of virulency, smacked of King Lear.

This quotation links the novel directly to the senseless and self-perpetuating violence and self-interest of Shakespeare's play. The similarities between the two texts are detailed and striking; the reduction of Lear to the animalistic and the brutal in his mad existence is evident in the plight of many of the characters residing at the Heights.

Themes

There are a number of ways in which *Wuthering Heights* can be seen to depend upon Shakespeare's tragedy. The two texts share a good deal of common ground in terms of themes. In its apparently senseless and frequently extreme brutality, its wild veering between sanity and insanity (and a profound probing of the boundaries between the two states), and its focus upon familial jealousy (between siblings and between parents and children), *Wuthering Heights* is closely connected to the trials and tribulations that befall the ill-fated King Lear. Both texts look closely at the implications of such individual behaviours and emotions for the body politic; in the case of *King Lear*, these are worked out on a national and international basis as well as on a more intimate and personal level, while in *Wuthering Heights* the effects are explored in a domestic scenario.

Location

Both *King Lear* and *Wuthering Heights* make extensive and essential use of a barren heath or moorland as a setting. In both texts this physical location is used to symbolise the emptiness and infertility of the lives of the characters and the situations in which they find themselves. The wildness of location is used in both texts to represent the wildness of passion and the brutal emotion that informs the characters' actions. It is vital to remember, however, that the wilderness also proves to be a place of recognition: it is a place where characters are forced to come face to face with the realities of their lives and to confront the frequently unpleasant personal truths they encounter there. Through his insanity and privations on the heath, Lear works his way towards a truer sense of value and the ultimate tragic reconciliation with his Cordelia. In much the same way, it is through the frightful 'madness' of their lives on the moors that the Earnshaws and the Lintons finally come to realise (in the figures of Catherine and Linton) the need and potential for true union between the families, untainted by ambition or revenge. Equally, Heathcliff, faced with the over-powering impact of his insane jealousy and hatred, feels the need for a reconciliation with himself and with Cathy, resulting in his apparently self-willed decline and death.

Storms

Storms play a significant symbolic role in both texts. A fearsome storm breaks after Lear has been thrown out of the houses of both Goneril and Regan, his daughters. The storm causes the hapless and foolish elderly king to reconsider his position and his actions, with the help of the loyal and trusted servants who remain with him. In the course of *Wuthering Heights* there are a number of significant storms: on Lockwood's second visit to the Heights he finds himself obliged to stay the night after being trapped by a snow storm. A second storm breaks with fury on the night that Heathcliff leaves his home at the Grange after overhearing Nelly Dean and Cathy discussing the issue of Cathy's marriage, and his return is also greeted by a heavy and storm-laden atmosphere of anticipation. These storms symbolise and externalise, among other things, the inner turmoil of the characters, familial division, insanity, anger, hatred, brutality and social upheaval. Both *King Lear* and *Wuthering Heights* depend to a considerable extent upon the metaphorical impact of these storms and the trials and tribulations they embody.

Names

There are two important coincidences of name between Shakespeare's play and Brontë's novel. The first is the name Edgar: in both the play and the novel Edgar is a well-meaning and loyal (and frequently naïve) character who finds himself caught up in a whirlwind of passionate events beyond his control. In *King Lear*, Edgar suffers at the hands of his younger, illegitimate brother Edmund, while in *Wuthering Heights*, Brontë's Edgar becomes the victim of Heathcliff. The comparisons that can be drawn between Edmund and Heathcliff are enlightening. It is significant that both men are wronged as a simple result of their questionable births; both suffer from the social stigma of illegitimacy (real or assumed), and as a result both develop into violent, vengeful and unprincipled men. While he is not known to be a bastard, as Edmund is, Heathcliff is nevertheless an outsider, an interloper into the family, and a man who has to fight for his social standing, all situations and disadvantages he shares with Edmund. Neither Edmund nor Heathcliff is ever fully accepted or acceptable, and as a result each resents his own position and that of the 'legitimate' and favoured Edgar, and both seek to establish themselves by skulduggery and underhand means.

The name of Heathcliff also resonates with Shakespeare's play in drawing together two of the most important locations in *King Lear* — the 'heath' where Lear finally degenerates into madness and is forced to recognise his foolishness, and the 'cliff' where the blinded Gloucester is deceived/saved by his son Edgar and finally comes to 'see' the naïvety which has led him to (mis)place his trust in the faithless Edmund. Both are key moments of personal awakening in the play, conferring great significance on these locations. It should be noted that the heath (Brontë's moors) and the cliff (Brontë's Penistone Crags, or indeed the Heights itself) are also highly significant locations in *Wuthering Heights*. It is not only in these locations that the characters of Brontë's novel undergo important experiences, however; it is through their contact with and response to Heathcliff himself that the characters come to a true and fuller, albeit painful, understanding of themselves. Heathcliff is like a barren landscape, as Cathy points out: a place of harshness and unforgiving brutality; a place of exposure and desolation.

Chapter summaries and notes

Although Brontë is not consistent in her naming of the two Catherines, for purposes of clarity in the following summaries, Cathy is used to denote the mother and Catherine the daughter.

Volume I, Chapter I

Mr Lockwood has rented Thrushcross Grange from Heathcliff. He is attempting to escape from society and from an unsuccessful relationship. He recounts a visit to

Wuthering Heights, Heathcliff's home. Heathcliff is introduced as an odd mixture of the gypsy and the gentleman, and he arouses in Lockwood feelings of both attraction and repulsion. His house is, tellingly, a dark and threatening place with fierce dogs and two strange servants, Joseph and Zillah.

This chapter introduces Lockwood's frame story; the reader sees the Heights as a place of brooding threat and casual violence.

Volume I, Chapter II

Lockwood pays a second visit to the Heights. He meets Catherine, whom he assumes to be Mrs Heathcliff. She treats him with suspicion and scorn. When Heathcliff arrives, Lockwood learns Catherine is the widow of Heathcliff's son. There is a violent snowstorm, and Lockwood finds himself unable to return to Thrushcross Grange. At the invitation of Zillah (he is ignored by everyone else) he agrees to stay the night.

The harsh weather of the moors is used to mirror the harshness of the inhabitants of the Heights.

Volume I, Chapter III

Zillah shows Lockwood to a chamber Heathcliff does not like to be occupied, though she does not know why. Once she has gone, Lockwood notices the names Catherine Earnshaw, Catherine Linton and Catherine Heathcliff scratched onto the window ledge. He reads Cathy's diary until he falls asleep, only to be haunted by nightmares: the first about a fanatical preacher, the second and more disturbing involving the ghost of Catherine Linton. He awakes screaming and Heathcliff enters, evidently disturbed and confused, unaware of Lockwood's presence. Lockwood leaves the room, but not before he sees Heathcliff in floods of tears begging 'Cathy' to come to him. The next morning Heathcliff walks Lockwood back to the Grange.

Cathy's diary is another narrative element within the text; already we have a proliferation of narrative voices. Early in the novel Brontë begins the doubling and deliberate confusion of character names by introducing the three Catherines. 'Cathy' and Heathcliff are connected in the reader's mind, and in the context of the supernatural.

Volume I, Chapter IV

Lockwood asks Ellen Dean (Nelly), his housekeeper, to tell him Heathcliff's story. Nelly begins by establishing the complex relationships between the inhabitants of the Heights, explaining that Catherine is the daughter of the late Catherine Linton ('Cathy'). She then begins her tale and the time frame of the novel moves back into the past, recounting how Mr Earnshaw, Cathy's father, returned to the Heights from a visit to Liverpool with Heathcliff, a starving, ragged street-child. Not entirely welcomed by the family, Heathcliff and Cathy nevertheless became very close companions. Cathy's brother, Hindley, comes particularly to dislike Heathcliff.

Nelly becomes the second narrator in the novel. Note Brontë's establishment of the relationships between Heathcliff and Cathy and Heathcliff and Hindley, which will be significant later.

Volume I, Chapter V

The widowed Earnshaw becomes increasingly irritable and spoils Heathcliff, his favourite. Hindley's dislike for Heathcliff grows, while the closeness between Heathcliff and Cathy deepens. Cathy demonstrates a manipulative and hard side to her character. Eventually Earnshaw dies.

Cathy and Heathcliff stand together against outside authority.

Volume I, Chapter VI

Hindley, the new owner of the Heights, marries Frances. He begins to maltreat Heathcliff systematically. Nelly recalls that one day Heathcliff recounted how, for amusement, he and Cathy spied on the Lintons, the inhabitants of Thrushcross Grange, to see how they lived there. They were caught and Cathy was bitten badly by a dog in trying to escape. The Lintons, disgusted by the wild manners of the children, drove Heathcliff away. Cathy, however, stayed at the Grange to recover, a visit encouraged and lengthened by Hindley out of his desire to separate her from Heathcliff.

Heathcliff becomes the third narrative voice of the novel. He is clearly entirely devoted to Cathy.

Volume I, Chapter VII

Nelly resumes the narrative. When Cathy returns to the Heights at Christmas, she has been transformed into a lady. She hurts Heathcliff by comparing him to Edgar Linton. In her absence he has been increasingly neglected. The next day, Heathcliff is not allowed to join the children's Christmas party and is banished to his room. Cathy joins him after the party. Heathcliff is determined to avenge himself on Hindley.

Distance begins to open up in the relationship between Cathy and Heathcliff. Cathy is caught between the desire to be with Heathcliff and the desire to be a lady with Edgar.

Volume I, Chapter VIII

Hareton, Hindley's son, is born. Frances dies soon after childbirth. Hindley grows desperate and falls into more and more dissolute ways. The Heights falls into violent confusion. The neighbours cease to visit, and Heathcliff becomes noticeably more savage and ferocious. Cathy continues to receive visits from Edgar Linton. During one such visit, they have a violent quarrel and Cathy behaves particularly badly and violently to both Edgar and Nelly. They reconcile their differences, however, and declare themselves lovers.

For the first time we see Cathy really behaving badly. This chapter provides a key point, as she chooses Edgar over Heathcliff. Brontë sets up an opposition between saint and devil.

Volume I, Chapter IX

Nelly tries to hide Hareton from Hindley, who returns home raging drunk. He catches her and threatens her with a knife, then dangles Hareton over the banisters. Hindley drops the child accidentally, but Heathcliff catches him, thus foiling his own desire for revenge. Later, Cathy tells Nelly that she has agreed to marry Edgar, neither knowing they are overheard by Heathcliff. She goes on to say that although she is uncertain about marrying Edgar, to marry Heathcliff would be degrading. Heathcliff runs away. Cathy becomes very ill after looking for Heathcliff in a violent storm, but he is nowhere to be found. Three years later she marries Edgar Linton. Nelly accompanies her to the Grange and Hareton is left alone with his increasingly brutish father.

'I am Heathcliff', Cathy remarks to Nelly, and she therefore abandons her true self in marrying Edgar Linton. The distance between Cathy and Heathcliff widens, although Cathy is convinced that they remain spiritually united.

Volume I, Chapter X

Heathcliff returns when Cathy and Edgar have been married for almost a year. He is changed: a tall, athletic man, apparently gentlemanly and educated. Cathy is delighted. He stays for tea and she learns that he is lodging at the Heights, winning large sums of money at gambling with Hindley. Heathcliff is a frequent visitor at the Grange and Isabella, Edgar's sister, becomes infatuated with him, much to Edgar's distress. Cathy warns Isabella against marrying Heathcliff.

Heathcliff, for all his surface changes, retains the old lurking brutality in his eyes. Cathy's use of violent natural analogies for his nature demonstrates her awareness and fears.

Volume I, Chapter XI

Heathcliff visits the Grange and kisses Isabella. This causes an argument between Cathy and Heathcliff, during which it becomes clear that he is using Isabella as a means of tormenting Cathy. Edgar becomes involved and strikes Heathcliff, who leaves to avoid further trouble. Cathy realises the extent to which she is trapped between Heathcliff and Edgar and vows to Nelly, when they are alone, that she will 'try to break their hearts by breaking my own'. When Edgar enters she throws a faked fit of frenzy.

The triangular relationship between Edgar, Cathy and Heathcliff grows ever more complex and destructive. Cathy's reactions are self-destructive and all-consuming.

Volume I, Chapter XII

After 3 days isolated in her room, Cathy calls for food and water. It becomes evident to Nelly that Cathy is delirious and believes she is back in her room at the Heights. She opens the window and talks to Heathcliff, who she imagines is there. Edgar becomes very concerned for her welfare. On her way to fetch the doctor, Nelly rescues Isabella's dog, which she finds hanging. Later she learns that Isabella and Heathcliff have eloped. Edgar refuses to rescue his sister.

In her delirium Cathy reverts to childhood (the reader wonders if she has ever really left it). Note the parallels between the window scene here and that in Volume I, Chapter III, when Heathcliff addresses the child ghost of Cathy. Edgar is guilty of a serious moral flaw in failing to rescue Isabella from Heathcliff.

Volume I, Chapter XIII

Two months pass and it is clear that Cathy will never recover. She is pregnant. Isabella and Heathcliff return to the Heights, but Edgar will still not relent. Isabella sends Nelly a letter describing the isolation, brutality and misery of her existence at the Heights. She regrets her marriage to Heathcliff bitterly.

Isabella's letter allows another narrative voice into the text. Even the gentle Isabella finds herself capable of violent emotion. Brontë presents us with the vulnerable position of women; without the help of her brother, she can do nothing to rectify the situation.

Volume I, Chapter XIV

Nelly visits Isabella. While at the Heights, she speaks to Heathcliff, telling him not to trouble Cathy any more. He refuses, claiming that Cathy loves him more than she loves her husband. Isabella and Heathcliff express their mutual hatred. Nelly agrees to carry a letter from Heathcliff to Cathy, under threat that he will break into the Grange if she does not comply.

Heathcliff despises Isabella because, knowing what he was, she still married him. While undeniably a romantic figure in the Byronic vein, he cannot be considered a conventional hero of romance.

Volume II, Chapter I

Nelly gives Cathy Heathcliff's letter. Cathy now appears beautiful in an unearthly, almost ghostly way. Heathcliff arrives and their reunion is bittersweet. Their conversation captures the complexities of peace and torment, acceptance and betrayal, love and revenge that characterise their relationship. Cathy knows she is dying and insists that Heathcliff stays. She faints and Heathcliff passes her body to Edgar, then leaves to await news.

This chapter forms a passionate emotional climax to the relationship between Cathy and Heathcliff. Nelly comments on what a 'strange and fearsome picture' they make. In its brutal, animalistic expression, their love appears to be a form of madness.

Volume II, Chapter II

Cathy gives birth to a daughter, Catherine, and dies 2 hours later. Nelly informs Heathcliff. He curses Cathy and begs her to haunt him so he will not be left without her. A few days after her death, when Edgar is absent, Heathcliff visits Cathy's body and exchanges a lock of Edgar's hair in her locket with one of his own. Nelly discovers this and symbolically encloses both locks of hair together. Cathy is buried in a lonely corner of the churchyard.

Heaven and hell are pitched against each other in the characters' views of where Cathy's spirit has sped. Heathcliff is convinced that she cannot exist peacefully beyond the grave without him.

Volume II, Chapter III

Isabella arrives at the Grange. She has run away from Heathcliff, and recounts to Nelly a tale of her husband's violence, born out of his agony over Cathy's death. She tells how Hindley attacked Heathcliff and was almost killed in the ensuing fight, and how the next morning she taunted Heathcliff so badly that he threw a knife at her. Isabella leaves, never to return to the neighbourhood again. (Later, in her new home, she gives birth to her son by Heathcliff, Linton, and dies 12 years later.) Six months after Cathy's death, Hindley dies, and Hareton is left in the care of Heathcliff, who is determined to wreak a posthumous revenge on Hindley by brutalising his son.

Isabella returns as a narrative voice. Consider the effects Brontë achieves through pairing characters in this chapter: Nelly/Hindley, Hindley/Heathcliff, Heathcliff/Cathy, Cathy/Isabella, Isabella/Hindley, Hareton/Linton, Heathcliff/Edgar.

Volume II, Chapter IV

Twelve years pass. Catherine grows up, seeming to combine the good qualities of both the Lintons and the Earnshaws. Her father keeps her within the park of the Grange, but she dreams of exploring further. Isabella falls ill and Edgar at last relents and goes to visit her. While he is away, Catherine deceives Nelly and goes exploring. Nelly eventually finds her safe at the Heights with her cousin Hareton. Heathcliff is not at home.

The novel returns suddenly from the adult world to the world of the child. The contrast is abrupt and harsh. The reader is tempted to see this as a second chance — will Catherine achieve happiness where her mother failed? The characteristics of the two are sufficiently similar to make the reader wary of such an interpretation.

Volume II, Chapter V

Isabella dies and Edgar returns to the Grange with Linton. That very evening, Joseph arrives from the Heights demanding that Linton be sent to Heathcliff, the boy's father.

A clear parallel is drawn between the arrival of Heathcliff from Liverpool with Earnshaw and the arrival of Linton with Edgar. There is an immediate contrast evident in the natures of Catherine and Linton, quite unlike the similarity between Cathy and Heathcliff as children.

Volume II, Chapter VI

The next morning Nelly takes Linton to the Heights. Linton learns for the first time about his father, as Isabella never spoke of him. Heathcliff and Joseph both show contempt for the delicate boy. Heathcliff, however, expresses his intention of looking after Linton, as he is the heir to the Grange, and he wishes him to survive at least until Edgar is dead.

Linton, like so many children in this novel, is abandoned in a cold and harsh environment (compare Heathcliff, Hindley, Hareton, Catherine).

Volume II, Chapter VII

Linton grows up to be a selfish and disagreeable young man, always complaining about his health. On Catherine's sixteenth birthday, she and Nelly stray on to Heathcliff's land. He invites them back to the Heights and tells Nelly he wants Catherine to marry Linton. Edgar learns of this visit and forbids Catherine to go there again. She begins a secret correspondence with Linton. Nelly discovers this, burns all the letters, and vows to tell Edgar if it continues.

The concept of trespassing is prevalent in this chapter — it links to the wider concerns of the novel and the Gothic genre in general.

Volume II, Chapter VIII

Edgar is confined to the house by illness. Catherine grows increasingly worried about being left alone when her father dies. Taking a walk with Nelly, Catherine becomes trapped outside the walls of the Grange park (a strange reversal of the images of imprisonment found elsewhere in the novel). Heathcliff finds her there and prompts her to pay another visit to the Heights to see Linton, whom he claims is dying of a broken heart. Nelly agrees to accompany her there.

Note the significance of the concepts of isolation and imprisonment.

Volume II, Chapter IX

Linton greets Catherine very ungraciously when she arrives. He is full of complaints and expresses his wish that Catherine should marry him. They argue about the relationship between husbands and wives in general and as displayed in the relationships between their respective parents. Catherine pushes Linton, making him cough so badly that she feels obliged to promise to return the next day. That night Nelly, who disapproves of going again to the Heights, catches a violent cold and is confined to her room. Catherine uses her evenings while both her father and Nelly are ill to continue her visits to Linton.

This chapter explores in depth the relationship between love and power which is central to the novel.

Volume II, Chapter X

Three weeks later, Nelly discovers what has been going on. Catherine recounts the sequence of her visits and we gain an impression of Linton as a manipulative invalid, prone to temper tantrums. We also hear of her inauspicious meetings with Hareton. Catherine's feelings for Linton are clearly based on sorrow and sympathy, not love. Nelly informs Edgar of Catherine's visits, and he forbids her to continue. He does, however, write to Linton, inviting him to visit the Grange.

Catherine joins the list of the novel's narrators. We see the stark differences between Catherine and Linton. We see that weakness and goodness cannot be equated carelessly.

Volume II, Chapter XI

Nelly suggests to Lockwood that he might become interested in Catherine, then returns to her narrative. Edgar admits to his worry about what will become of Catherine should he die. He writes to Linton, asking to see him, but Heathcliff refuses to allow Linton to visit the Grange. Edgar will not consent to Catherine visiting the Heights, but eventually concedes to a meeting on the moor, with Nelly's supervision. Edgar wishes Catherine to marry Linton so she will not have to leave the Grange when he dies.

Catherine's vulnerable position as an unmarried female is emphasised.

Volume II, Chapter XII

Nelly and Catherine ride out to meet Linton. They very nearly reach the Heights before they find him. He is evidently very ill. He finds conversation difficult, but will not allow Catherine to go, as he is obviously afraid of his father, whom we suspect is watching the meeting from some vantage point. Catherine half-heartedly agrees to stay.

We see the extent of Heathcliff's manipulative cruelty towards his son. The energy, life and power of Heathcliff provide a stark contrast to the pathetic weakness of Linton.

Volume II, Chapter XIII

A week later the visit is repeated. Edgar is much worse, and Catherine does not wish to go, but Edgar insists. Catherine, angry at having to leave her own father, is disgusted by Linton's admissions of terror of his father. Heathcliff appears and asks Nelly how long Edgar is likely to live, as he is worried Linton may die before Edgar. He orders Linton to take Catherine into the Heights and forces Nelly in too. He locks them in, then brutally makes it clear that they will not be allowed out until Catherine and Linton are married. Nelly and Catherine are separated, and Nelly remains imprisoned for 5 days, unaware of what has happened to Catherine.

Brontë emphasises Heathcliff's dominance and tyrannical power, as well as Catherine's unprotected position as a single woman.

Volume II, Chapter XIV

On the fifth day of her captivity, Nelly is released by Zillah. She is allowed to return to the Grange, and Catherine is to follow in time for Edgar's funeral. He is not yet dead, but soon will be. On her return to the Grange, Nelly sends a rescue party to release Catherine, but the men come away without her, fooled by Heathcliff's lies. Very early the next morning, however, Catherine returns by herself, having forced Linton to help her escape. Edgar dies 'blissfully', unaware of Catherine's marriage to Linton.

Edgar has died before safe-guarding changes can be made to his will. Heathcliff acquires ever greater powers and property.

Volume II, Chapter XV

Heathcliff collects Catherine from the Grange to take care of Linton, in whom Heathcliff no longer has any interest. Heathcliff, in a very strange mood, tells Nelly that, the night before, he bribed the sexton to uncover Cathy's coffin so he could see her face again. Dissuaded from this, he struck out the side of her coffin and bribed the sexton to put his body in with Cathy's when he dies. He explains that Cathy's spirit has haunted him night and day since she died. He goes on to tell how, on the night of her burial, he dug up her coffin to embrace her one last time. Ever since then he has been sure of her 'living' presence with him, both comforting and tormenting him.

The emphasis is on the profundity and grotesqueness of Cathy and Heathcliff's continued relationship, highlighting the role of the supernatural in the novel. Heathcliff envisages both a bodily (though not sexual) and spiritual unity with Cathy.

Volume II, Chapter XVI

Nelly's narrative has now almost reached the present. Heathcliff refuses to allow a doctor to be called for Linton. Finally Linton dies, and Catherine is left destitute, as her husband has left everything to Heathcliff in his will. One day when Heathcliff is out, Catherine comes downstairs. Hareton, sorry for her, makes friendly advances. He wishes her to read to him and to teach him to read, as he is illiterate. She refuses harshly.

As so often in the novel, revenge for wrong is exacted not on the perpetrator, but on an innocent party — here, Hareton suffers for Heathcliff's actions.

Volume II, Chapter XVII

Lockwood visits the Heights to end his tenancy at the Grange. He gives Catherine a note from Nelly. Hareton tries to take it to Heathcliff, but seeing her upset does not do so. She cannot reply to the letter as she has no paper and no books to write on. She mocks Hareton, the only possessor of books in the household — Heathcliff uses them to torment him with his ignorance. He fetches the books for Catherine, but then slaps her when she persists in her cruel mockery of him. Lockwood concludes his business with Heathcliff and stays for a meal.

Books play an important role in the relationship between Hareton and Catherine. Look at the relationship in the novel between knowledge and ignorance.

Volume II, Chapter XVIII

It is the autumn of 1802, and Lockwood, in the vicinity on a hunting trip, returns to the Grange. He finds it almost deserted, and Nelly removed to the Heights. He goes to the Heights to see what has changed, and finds Catherine teaching Hareton, now well dressed, how to read. The lesson is interspersed with kisses and kind words. Nelly is pleased to see Lockwood and tells him how a fortnight after he left the Grange, she was summoned by Heathcliff to the Heights to keep Catherine out of his way. She recounts the ending of the animosity between Catherine and Hareton, hastened by Hareton's injury in a shooting accident.

The relationship between Hareton and Catherine indicates the unity of the houses of Earnshaw and Linton, the Heights and the Grange. Heathcliff's relinquishment of power and control begins.

Volume II, Chapter XIX

The next day a conflict arises between Heathcliff and Catherine. Hareton finds himself caught in the middle of his fear for Heathcliff and his love for Catherine. Heathcliff unexpectedly backs out of the confrontation. He is struck by the resemblance between Hareton, Catherine and Cathy. He no longer takes any interest in everyday life, but is totally absorbed with Cathy and his memories. He tells Nelly that he no longer feels part of the living world, as he is so close to that of the dead or the immortal.

Heathcliff sees and feels Cathy in everything — he is incapable of relating to anything except in the terms of his relationship to her. This is Brontë's perception of true haunting.

Volume II, Chapter XX

Heathcliff all but stops eating and spends all night out walking. He becomes increasingly disengaged from the real world, and claims to be within sight of his heaven. He expresses the desire to settle his affairs with his lawyer. When Nelly reminds him of the need to think of his soul, he informs her that he has his own heaven, which has nothing to do with the heaven of Christian teaching. He refuses to see a doctor and the next morning is found dead at the open window of his room. He is buried as he requested by the sexton. In the vicinity regular sightings of the ghosts of Cathy and Heathcliff are reported. Catherine and Hareton are to be married and leave the Heights for the Grange. The novel ends with Lockwood's visit to the churchyard, where he sees the three graves of Edgar, Cathy and Heathcliff.

Brontë concludes the novel with symbolic reunions in the coming marriage of Catherine and Hareton, which will reunite the two houses, and the burial of Heathcliff, which brings him back to his Cathy. Note the final images of the crumbling wilderness of the churchyard.

Characters and pairings

Brontë's use of Gothic stereotypes

In beginning to consider the characters of the novel, it is as well to remember that *Wuthering Heights* is a text working with (if not exactly within) the parameters of the Gothic genre (see pp. 11–16). Any genre develops its own typical features and its own particular requirements. In the following passage from his book *The Literature of Terror*, David Punter writes on the stereotypical characters of Gothic novels:

> The world in which it did deal was peopled with stock characters, who discoursed in predictable ways: the shy, nervous, retiring heroine, who was nevertheless usually possessed of a remarkable ability to survive hideously dangerous situations; the heavy-handed, tyrannical father; the cast of comic extras and servants who, like many of the other characters, often seem to be lifted wholesale out of Jacobean drama; and above all the villain. The villain was always the most complex and interesting character in Gothic fiction, even when drawn with a clumsy hand: awe-inspiring, endlessly resourceful in pursuit of his often opaquely evil ends, and yet possessed of a mysterious attractiveness, he stalks from the pages of one Gothic novel to another, manipulating the doom of others while the knowledge of his own eventual fate surrounds him like the monastic habit and cowl which he so often wore.

A comparison of the main figures of the novel against these ideas is essential in beginning to understand how Brontë's characterisation works with and differs from the generic norm. You need to think carefully about the characters of *Wuthering Heights,* and to consider how far Punter's outline of stereotypes applies to your understanding of them. It is also important to evaluate the extent to which it may be considered a fair reflection of Emily Brontë's use of character in the novel.

Heathcliff

Heathcliff consistently proves himself to be an unprincipled and tyrannical villain. He can without question be considered an awe-inspiring man, a fact attested to by the absolute fear he inspires in most of the other characters in the novel and by the power he holds over the reader. The complexity of his nature and an attendant air of mystery are central to the power of Brontë's delineation of him as he, to borrow Punter's phrase, stalks the pages of the novel. He proves adept in manipulating the fate of those around him, turning their lives and their property to his own purposes and taking a villainous glee in the pain he inflicts. Again, like Punter's stereotypical villain, he is fully aware of his own fate — the long-desired reunion with his beloved Cathy.

Heathcliff is no simple villain, however. As Punter observes, the villain of Gothic is frequently 'possessed of a mysterious attractiveness'. Like a number of the characters within the novel, we find ourselves undeniably attracted to Heathcliff, who has about him something of the dash and fire of the Byronic hero. There exists around him a perpetual aura of mystery — what are his true roots? Where did he go and what did he do during his absence from the neighbourhood of the Heights and the Grange? Yet it is not mystery alone that attracts the reader. Sympathy also has a role to play; an outsider from the moment he arrives in Yorkshire, Heathcliff never gains acceptance and is frequently maltreated by those who should care for him. Forever reminded of his dubious birth, background and social status, he is forced into a corner where he has no choice but to defend himself ferociously. Like Ambrosio in Matthew Lewis's *The Monk*, one of the first and greatest Gothic villains, and like the monster in Mary Shelley's *Frankenstein*, Heathcliff is an abandoned child, a victim as well as a villain.

Brontë's women

None of Brontë's women can truly be considered conventionally shy and retiring. The frail and innocent Gothic stereotype is not a presence in the world of *Wuthering Heights*. Cathy, Catherine and Isabella are all delineated as strong, forthright women who do not remain passive in the face of danger, but react, often with considerable power, to defend themselves, frequently provoking worse danger in so doing. Isabella comes the closest to Punter's stereotypical outline, eventually fleeing the wrath of Heathcliff and the disapproval of her brother, Edgar, to live out her life in exile in the south. However, she does not do this without having faced considerable, even life-threatening, brutality at the hands of Heathcliff, so it is difficult to compare her to the likes of Emily St Auber (in *The Mysteries of Udolpho* by Ann Radcliffe), Antonia (in *The Monk* by Matthew Lewis) and a host of other typical Gothic females.

Cathy and Catherine are still less typical of this role. Neither can be considered in any sense a traditionally 'weak' Gothic female. Cathy is in many ways the driving force behind the villainy and the nature of Heathcliff, and as such could even be seen to share something of the role of the villain, while Catherine is stoical in the face of Heathcliff's machinations and brutality, becoming distinctly brutalised herself until she finds salvation in her relationship with Hareton towards the end of the novel.

Nelly Dean

The devoted nurse is a standard figure of Gothic fiction (see texts such as *The Nurse's Tale* by Elizabeth Gaskell and *The Turn of the Screw* by Henry James for other examples).

Joseph and Zillah

These two characters fulfil the role of the comic servants; as the reader rapidly comes to see, however, they are no amusingly benign presence, but take on a peculiarly dark role in the text. Brontë uses them as the source of much black humour.

The characters of *Wuthering Heights* can therefore be seen to fulfil several of the key elements outlined by Punter. The relationship of the characters to the stereotypes of Gothic is not straightforward, however; Brontë adopts some of the stock elements of Gothic characters, but adapts them to her own ends.

Doubling of characters

The doubling of characters and names is a device employed frequently throughout the novel. We soon note that names are repeated in each generation of the two families. Through this device Brontë creates a deliberately confusing and complex set of interrelations within the framework of the novel. The uncertainties this generates for the reader frequently echo the doubt and insecurity of the characters themselves. It also links to one of the most significant components of Gothic fiction — the fear (and the apparent inevitability) of generational repetition. We are repeatedly brought face to face with the extent to which violence and characteristics descend from one generation to another in the world of the Earnshaws and the Lintons.

In the course of the novel, Emily Brontë, like Mary Shelley in *Frankenstein*, Robert Louis Stevenson in *Dr Jekyll and Mr Hyde*, and many other authors of Gothic, makes extensive use of pairs of characters. These pairings are not necessarily fixed; indeed, they frequently shift as the novel progresses, creating a range of differing effects, pointing out both similarities and differences between the characters who are paired. The following pairings are all highly significant. The most important pairing of all, that of Cathy and Heathcliff, is dealt with separately on pages 41–45.

Lockwood and Heathcliff

Lockwood and Heathcliff are paired in our imagination by the newly arrived Lockwood: '…Mr Heathcliff and I are such a suitable pair to divide the desolation between us' (p. 3). We may assume initially that this indicates a similarity between the two men. However, it quickly becomes apparent that Lockwood is actually pointing to the profound divisions between himself and his landlord: Lockwood represents gentility and the acceptable, as opposed to Heathcliff, who, while technically a gentleman, is an 'upstart' and distinctly lacking in gentility. They form the last in a long line of oppositions between the householders of the Heights and the Grange.

Cathy and Catherine

Cathy and Catherine share many characteristics. Both are independent in spirit and are capable of great personal strength, as well as being perpetrators of psychological cruelty. Their lives and marriages parallel one another significantly. Catherine appears to be a more controlled version of her mother. She is, after all, a combination of Earnshaw and Linton blood. The reader sees Catherine's life as, in a sense, a second chance at happiness after the sad dissatisfaction of Cathy's. This is suggested structurally within the novel itself, the second half of the book (subsequent to the death of Cathy) substantially reflecting the first half.

Heathcliff and Hindley

Heathcliff and Hindley are in many ways reflections of each other. Hindley deliberately and systematically maltreats Heathcliff after the death of Mr Earnshaw, because of his apparent resentment that Heathcliff, the socially suspect outsider, has been accepted into the Earnshaw household. As a result, Heathcliff is determined to avenge himself upon Hindley. As so often in the novel, revenge is sought not upon the perpetrator, but on the perpetrator's representative. In this instance it is Hareton, Hindley's son, who is made to suffer as Heathcliff uses the same techniques as were used against him to deliberately brutalise Hareton and the Earnshaw name.

Heathcliff and Hareton

Heathcliff is made into a brute by the treatment of Hindley, and so, in his turn, Hareton is made into a brute by Heathcliff. There is a grudging respect between them in their similarity.

Heathcliff and Linton

Both Heathcliff and Linton come to the world of the Heights as outsiders. Heathcliff is brought back from Liverpool by Earnshaw and Linton is brought back from the south by Edgar after Isabella's death. Both have a natural ability to manipulate. They are clearly opposites too: Heathcliff is a fit, powerful and domineering man, while Linton is sickly, weak and easily dominated. Linton lacks his father's saving graces — Heathcliff does not appear naturally unpleasant, but is made so.

Heathcliff and Edgar

Heathcliff and Edgar are rivals for Cathy's hand. They are distinct opposites: Heathcliff is wild, a risk-taker and passionate in both love and hate; Edgar is cultivated, always errs on the side of safety, and is usually restrained in his emotional reactions. They are strangely united, however, in their life-long rivalry (we may even say enmity) over Cathy, the focus of which is transferred to the desire to possess the Grange and Catherine after Cathy has died. This profound connection is emphasised in the final image of their graves at the end of the novel.

Linton and Hareton

Throughout the novel Linton and Hareton are presented as opposites. Linton is a weak, unpleasant, manipulative, mean, unhelpful and selfish youth; Hareton, on the other hand, is seen to be resilient, capable of warmth, frank, straightforward, naturally kind and helpful, and often thinks of others. Both appear, in a sense, as 'sons' of Heathcliff.

Catherine Linton/Catherine Earnshaw/Catherine Heathcliff

Brontë deliberately sets up a confusion over identity early in the novel, by the multiple repetition of the name Catherine. Lockwood sleeps for a night in the haunted chamber at the Heights and finds scratched into the wood of the disturbingly claustrophobic bed the three names of Catherine Linton, Catherine Earnshaw and Catherine Heathcliff. Unsurprisingly, his immediate reaction is one of bewilderment.

The effect on the reader is much the same as that on Lockwood. Like the hapless narrator, we find ourselves plunged into the unfamiliar and deeply distressing world of the Heights. The uncertainty established by the three names serves to deepen this. It throws us immediately into the world of confusion and malaise that characterises the novel and allows us to share something of Lockwood's uncertainty and difficulty. The names represent the concept of generational repetition that is to be so important to the text, both literally and conceptually. They also alert the reader to the important idea of the divided personality (see the Freudian reading of the novel on pages 80–82) and to the often uncertain distinction between characters in Brontë's fictional world. Such a view is strengthened when the reader considers that both Cathy and Catherine may be said to hold each of these three names in the course of the tale. This draws attention to the close (almost inextricable) links between the households of Earnshaw and Linton, and the problematic interloper Heathcliff. Placed in the context of the haunting visit of the child-ghost of Cathy, we inevitably link these names with events of the supernatural and/or evil.

Doubling of plot devices

It is not only through the pairing of characters that Brontë achieves her effect; it is also through the pairing of events. In one sense this may be seen as a natural progression of her extensive doubling of character; the deep similarities and contrasts that exist between the characters are frequently revealed by their exposure to the same or similar circumstances. This naturally emphasises the significant issue of generational repetition (and the fear of it), a concern addressed repeatedly within the Gothic genre, as Laura Kranzler has identified in her discussion of the Gothic tales of Elizabeth Gaskell (see page 77). In such a reading of the text, the repetition of events would seem to emphasise the unchangeable and unchanging brutality and self-destruction of the households of Linton and Earnshaw.

Such a view is undoubtedly significant. However, the reader needs to remember that repetition can lead to improvement. This is also important to *Wuthering Heights*, as it encourages the reader to hope for change. Structurally, the novel may be seen to fall into two halves — the story of Cathy, Edgar and Heathcliff told in the first, and the balancing tale of Catherine, Hareton and Linton in the second. While we remain aware of the similarities between the mother and the daughter, and the strange triangular relationships in which they find themselves, we always remain alert to the possibility that we might witness in the life of Catherine a second chance — the victory of hope, fulfilment and happiness where the life of her mother was only sadness and disappointment.

Brontë holds both of these potential outcomes carefully in the balance, maintaining a high level of uncertainty in the reader right until the end. Heathcliff and Edgar remain alive throughout both halves of the tale and are active players in both, as is Cathy, arguably, from beyond the grave. The fates of both the older generation and the younger generation are locked together through Brontë's mirroring of events and motifs such as locks of hair, window scenes, the repetition of brutality, the cycle of vengeance and repeated threats from the outsider (Heathcliff/Linton).

Character sketches

When approaching any work of fiction, it is essential to draw together your thoughts about key characters and their role within the text. The following list suggests the main areas for consideration:

- Why have they been included?
- How do they connect to the themes and concerns of the novel as a whole?

- How do they relate to those around them?
- How do they use language? How do they act?
- How do others act towards them and speak about them?

With the exception of Heathcliff (dealt with on pages 41–49), suggested areas for consideration of the central characters in *Wuthering Heights* are outlined below.

Cathy

The following quotations all shed light on the character of Cathy.

(1)   Certainly, she had ways with her such as I never saw a child take up before; and she put all of us past our patience fifty times and oftener in a day: from the hour she came down stairs, till the hour she went to bed, we had not a minute's security that she wouldn't be in mischief. Her spirits were always at high-water mark, her tongue always going — singing, laughing, and plaguing everybody who would not do the same. A wild, wick slip she was — but, she had the bonniest eye, and sweetest smile, and lightest foot in the parish; and, after all, I believe she meant no harm; for when once she made you cry in good earnest, it seldom happened that she would not keep you company, and oblige you to be quiet that you might comfort her. (p. 42)

This is the reader's first detailed introduction to the character of Cathy. She is immediately presented as an emotionally volatile and passionate child. She is profoundly dedicated to Heathcliff. She is also seen to be a deeply selfish child always desiring attention; she is wild and wicked (the potential for cruelty and violence surely hinted at in her ability to make others cry), full of energy and likes to be in control. She is mischievous and continually annoying to others. At the same time, however, her beauty is emphasised, as befits the heroine of a romance or a Gothic novel.

(2)   In the place where she heard Heathcliff termed a 'vulgar young ruffian,' and 'worse than a brute,' she took care not to act like him; but at home she had small inclination to practise politeness that would only be laughed at, and restrain an unruly nature when it would bring her neither credit, nor praise. (p. 67)

This extract illustrates not only Cathy's duplicitous and deceitful nature, but also something of the ambiguous nature of her relationship with Heathcliff. It suggests the coming complexity of the romance between the two, as well as the similarly 'unruly nature' they share.

(3)   ...she seemed to allow herself such wide latitude, that I had little faith in her principles, and still less sympathy for her feelings. (p. 107)

Noteworthy here is the wild and uncontrollable element in Cathy's character. She seems unable to manage herself and her behaviour completely — especially in regard to Heathcliff.

(4)   '...remind him of my passionate temper, verging, when kindled, on frenzy — I wish you
        could dismiss that apathy out of your countenance, and look rather more anxious about me!'
        (p. 117)

This demonstrates Cathy's vengeful and controlling nature. She wishes to
manipulate both her husband and Nelly, and presents herself as unstable almost to
the point of insanity. This passage also illustrates how extremely selfish Cathy can
be in the way she demands Nelly's sympathy at the end of the section.

(5)   It was enough to try the patience of a saint, such senseless, wicked rages! There she lay
        dashing her head against the arm of the sofa, and grinding her teeth, so that you might
        fancy she would crash them to splinters! (p. 118)

This shows the extent to which Cathy will go in her determination to manipulate Edgar
and Nelly. Again, it suggests Cathy's questionable sanity, especially as her frenzy is
an act for the benefit of her 'audience', in an attempt to control her husband.

(6)   Tossing about, she increased her feverish bewilderment to madness, and tore the pillow with
        her teeth, then raising herself up all burning, desired that I would open the window. (p. 122)

Cathy seemingly adopts madness at will, a fact revealed by the previous extract as
well as this one. Look at how the passage develops in the ensuing paragraphs,
however, where the insanity appears more genuine — we are left uncertain whether
it is real or not. Many things in the novel border on the insane — Cathy's behaviour
reflects this.

(7)   The flash of her eyes had been succeeded by a dreamy and melancholy softness: they no
        longer gave the impression of looking at the objects around her; they appeared always to
        gaze beyond, and far beyond — you would have said out of this world... (p. 158)

This passage emphasises the 'decay' of Cathy; the fire and passion of her nature,
which we have seen repeatedly throughout the novel, seem now to have expired,
to be replaced by an unmistakeable aura of other-worldliness; her mental stability
comes under question once more, as she is evidently no longer able to focus her
attention on the world around her, but rather appears to be distanced from rationality and her own mind. This passage serves to evoke sympathy in the reader, and
also wins our affection for Cathy in her strange, supernatural and 'unearthly'
beauty.

Hindley

Hindley is presented as a desperate, reckless, tyrannical, greedy, lonely, vengeful,
bullying, evil and frequently drunken man. After his wife's death, Hindley's

character darkens further, undergoing a sudden and dramatic shift typical of Gothic fiction. Cathy says of him: 'Hindley is too reckless to select his acquaintance prudently' (p. 99). Further on, she adds: 'doubtless my brother's covetousness will prompt him to accept the terms [of Heathcliff's return to the Grange]; he was always greedy, though what he grasps with one hand, he flings away with the other' (pp. 99–101).

Linton

Linton is a fundamentally weak and pathetic character. He is a manipulative and shameless youth, always willing to use his physical condition as a means of attaining his own selfish ends. In spite of this, however, Brontë does manage to create some sympathy in the reader for him. Linton is bullied repeatedly and mercilessly by his father and used by him as a means of winning the estate of the Grange through marrying him to Catherine. In the face of such maltreatment Linton is helpless, a lonely and pathetically fearful figure. According to Heathcliff he is a 'whelp' and 'tin polished to ape a service of silver'; Nelly is no more favourably impressed with him, believing him to be a 'selfish and disagreeable' young man. She comments too on the wilful perversity of his nature, calling him 'an indulged plague of a child', who is twisted and unnatural.

Isabella

Isabella is perhaps the weakest of the women Brontë presents her reader with, although she arguably suffers the most at the hands of Heathcliff. She proves herself to be naïve and headstrong, refusing to accept the advice of Nelly, Cathy and her brother, Edgar, on the issue of marrying Heathcliff. This arises from a fundamentally romantic (and Romantic) view of life, which leads her into self-deluding fantasies. Her choices leave her a shattered and maltreated woman, abandoned by both husband and brother, and profoundly isolated.

Catherine

Catherine is in many ways very similar to Cathy: she is a beautiful young woman, 'high spirited, but not rough'. She is sensitive and lively, with the 'capacity for intense attractions'. This latter characteristic proves to be both her undoing and her salvation. It initially leaves her open to Heathcliff's greedy machinations, which he pursues via his son, Linton. She is radically changed by her contact with Linton and Heathcliff, turning slowly and surely into the harridan we see in the scenes at the Heights. In her later relationship with Hareton, however, she finds a suitable companion and a fruitful outlet for the loving side of her character.

Hareton

Hareton is presented as a fearless and endlessly resilient young man. His brutalisation, Heathcliff's revenge on Hindley, leaves him illiterate and unable to express himself; this makes him angry and so, at times, he finds his only means of communication and his only vent for frustration in physical violence. Despite his deliberate maltreatment of him, Heathcliff remains alive to Hareton's fundamentally good and noble nature, describing him as 'gold put to the use of paving stones'. This prepares the reader for the change that is to occur in Hareton later, once he has established a relationship with Catherine — we see him as a proud man, but one capable of improvement. He changes significantly after Catherine alters her attitude towards him, and we see the beneficial effect of education. Nelly informs the reader that:

> His honest, warm, and intelligent nature shook off rapidly the clouds of ignorance and degradation in which it had been bred; and Catherine's sincere commendations acted as a spur to his industry. His brightening mind brightened his features, and added spirit and nobility to their aspect — I could hardly fancy it the same individual... (p. 322)

Joseph

Joseph is a cruel, cold-hearted, religious hypocrite, and Heathcliff's faithful servant.

Zillah

Zillah is another loyal servant at the Heights; quieter and less apparently cruel than Joseph, she nevertheless does nothing to try to help the victims of Heathcliff's barbarity.

Nelly Dean

Nelly Dean is a dedicated family servant. She finds herself repeatedly torn between the warring factions within the tale, but bravely refuses to give up the middle ground she inhabits, despite suffering for it both emotionally and physically. In her role as the primary narrator of the tale, she provides the reader with an overview of the unfolding events, offering a rationalising commentary. She has clearly been both deeply affected and deeply scarred by what has taken place at the Grange and at Wuthering Heights — she has watched the steady disintegration and resurrection of the Earnshaw and Linton families over a long period of time.

She is the repository of all the characters' secrets. Cathy and Heathcliff both confide in her and make her the bearer of their emotional baggage. She is repeatedly put in impossible positions, frequently finding herself imprisoned (sometimes literally) within her divided loyalties. Her common-sense, no-nonsense viewpoint counterbalances the excesses and passions of the main characters and roots the novel in reality.

Cathy and Heathcliff

The most striking and extensive of the pairings Brontë uses in the course of the novel is that between Cathy and Heathcliff. In *Frankenstein* Shelley makes use of the concept of the doppelgänger, pairing Frankenstein and his monster, and in *Wuthering Heights* the relationship between Cathy and Heathcliff functions in a similar way. The two characters are allied so closely as to appear virtually complementary halves of the same character.

Throughout the novel, Brontë is at pains to emphasise the extreme closeness that exists between Cathy and Heathcliff. They prove incapable of living without one another, but also peculiarly unable to coexist happily. They are, in many ways, destructively alike — their temperaments and psychologies are so similar that they connect perfectly, but for that very reason cannot combine. Theirs is a relationship divided between love and hate, the desire to possess and the desire to break free, the need to heal and the need to wound. The relationship is never consummated physically, nor is it even romantically physical (although brute physical contact does have an important role to play); rather it is deeply spiritual. The extreme nature of the relationship and the emotions of both Cathy and Heathcliff are central to its impact on the reader, as are the excessive claims of the nature of their unity. On the whole, it is an unfulfilled relationship — even when they are reunited in death, the relationship is somehow 'unholy' and incomplete, in that their spirits cannot rest.

Examples and analysis

(1)   'If all else perished, and *he* remained, I should still continue to be; and, if all else remained, and he were annihilated, the Universe would turn to a mighty stranger. I should not seem a part of it. My love for Linton is like the foliage in the woods. Time will change it, I'm well aware, as winter changes the trees — my love for Heathcliff resembles the eternal rocks beneath — a source of little visible delight, but necessary. Nelly, I *am* Heathcliff — he's always, always in my mind — not as a pleasure, any more than I am always a pleasure to myself — but, as my own being — so, don't talk of our separation again...' (pp. 82–83)

Cathy here betrays the extreme emotion that embodies her relationship with Heathcliff. Their relationship is presented in elemental and absolute terms; as something enduring, hard and unchangeable. Their union is spiritual — the kind that is later to be fulfilled beyond the grave when they are reunited in death. The language Brontë employs conveys strikingly the power of feeling that exists within Cathy here. Her sense of herself and her worth are entirely bound up with Heathcliff, to the point that she defines her very existence by him: 'I *am* Heathcliff'. The reader must note, however, that the extreme closeness of their relationship is no source of happiness to her. There is 'little visible delight' in their relationship, a fact that becomes all too painfully clear as the novel progresses, and is frequently a source of great torment to both Cathy and Heathcliff.

(2) Cathy describes Heathcliff as 'my all in all' (p. 125). This emphasises further the extent to which Cathy and Heathcliff depend upon one another. Their devotion to and their dependence on each other is total. The removal of her 'all' when she marries Edgar has a profound effect upon Cathy, as it does upon Heathcliff. Similarly, their second separation, when Cathy dies, condemns both to unrest and heart-rending sorrow. When this happens, Cathy and Heathcliff suffer extremely, in keeping with the extreme nature of their relationship, as they have lost the greater part of themselves in losing the other.

(3) 'It's a rough journey, and a sad heart to travel it; and we must pass by Gimmerton Kirk, to go that journey! We've braved its ghosts often together, and dared each other to stand among the graves and ask them to come.... But Heathcliff, if I dare you now, will you venture? If you do, I'll keep you. I'll not lie there by myself; they may bury me twelve feet deep, and throw the church down over me; but I won't rest till you are with me.... I never will!' (p. 126)

This is one of a number of passages where clear links are established with the earlier window scene, when Heathcliff calls after the spirit of Cathy from the window of the Heights after Lockwood's nightmare. The connection between Cathy and Heathcliff is an eternal one; they are tied together by such powerful spiritual bonds that they can be said literally to haunt one another. Cathy clearly intimates that until they are reunited in death, no form of completion or closure will be possible. Note too the way in which Cathy drives Heathcliff on; it is at her insistence that he undertakes the dare to enter the churchyard and call up the spirits. In the same way, it will be as a result of her continual visitations after her death that he will eventually find himself pulled back into union with her. Cathy's determination and force of character is clear in the language she uses, as she envisages herself buried at double the conventional depth and covered by the weight of the entire church. Such language is fully in keeping with the extreme nature of her character and the powerful emotions she feels toward Heathcliff.

(4) In her eagerness she rose, and supported herself on the arm of the chair. At that earnest appeal, he turned to her, looking absolutely desperate. His eyes wide, and wet, at last, flashed fiercely on her; his breast heaved convulsively. An instant they held asunder; and then how they met I hardly saw, but Catherine made a spring, and he caught her, and they were locked in an embrace from which I thought my mistress would never be released alive. In fact, to my eyes, she seemed directly insensible. He flung himself into the nearest seat, and on my approaching hurriedly to ascertain if she had fainted, he gnashed at me, and foamed like a mad dog, and gathered her to him with greedy jealousy. I did not feel as if I were in the company of a creature of my own species... (p. 162)

This, one of the great 'romantic' scenes of the novel, offers a number of useful insights into the relationship between Cathy and Heathcliff. The reader is initially struck by the brutality and power of the coming together of the two 'lovers'. It is more like a battle between wild beasts than a meeting of passion. Throughout the passage, the vocabulary Brontë employs indicates excess and uncontrollable emotion.

Cathy seems to be taken beyond the realms of human emotion. Nelly believes her to have passed out, and fears that the shock of such a meeting may literally kill her. Even in her frail condition at this point, however, Cathy is capable of sudden and violent physical action in Heathcliff's presence, springing into his arms.

Heathcliff is presented as a greedy animal, determined to wrench every ounce of experience from this meeting with Cathy. He is the victim of a wordless passion — both he and Cathy here express their feelings physically rather than verbally. He is clearly at the borders of sanity, as Brontë suggests when she compares him to 'a mad dog', and even appears questionably human. Readers of Bram Stoker's *Dracula* may be struck by the apparent similarity between Heathcliff and the Count, who is often animal-like in his predatory relations with a sequence of women, and who takes on the shape of a wolf at will. Dogs are central to the Gothic tale *The Hounds of the Baskervilles*, by Conan Doyle, too.

Similarities

Although they are in many respects so close, Cathy and Heathcliff are also significantly different and do much to hurt each other. The need to wound, which forms such a striking element within their relationship, seems to spring from its impossibility. The infliction of pain, both psychological and physical, which constantly marks their relationship, is highly significant for the reader, as it represents an almost pathological need in both Cathy and Heathcliff to be hurt and to be punished. There seems to be a mutual, unexpressed recognition of the fact that their relationship cannot be allowed to flourish along conventionally established lines; marriage and domesticity would suit the needs of neither, nor would it be sustainable, the reader feels, given the nature of the two individuals involved and the exceptional passions they embody. The morally uncertain world of the novel and the moral uncertainty of Cathy and Heathcliff cannot allow for the perfect unity of souls that they seem to desire. As Cathy states in her discussion with Nelly Dean, union with Heathcliff and marriage to him are two entirely distinct issues; while she freely admits the extent of her passion for him and the extreme personal closeness that exists between them, she cannot and will not bring herself to marry him. She makes this clear to Nelly:

'It would degrade me to marry Heathcliff, now; so he shall never know how I love him; and that, not because he's handsome, Nelly, but because he's more myself than I am. Whatever our souls are made of, his and mine are the same, and Linton's is as different as a moonbeam from lightning, or frost from fire.' (p. 81)

The comparisons she draws between her nature and those of Heathcliff and Edgar are telling, and reveal the centrality of the similar natures of Heathcliff and Cathy within the novel.

> 'I wish I could hold you,' she continued, bitterly, 'till we were both dead! I shouldn't care what you suffered. I care nothing for your sufferings. Why shouldn't you suffer? I do!' (p. 160)

This short extract indicates the fierce, vindictive and impulsive love that abides between Cathy and Heathcliff. Her wish that he should die at her hands suggests the extent to which he infuriates and angers her. It also reveals, however, a deep yearning for their continued togetherness; she wishes to cleave to him so that they may never be separated. The contradictory impressions thus created illustrate the complicated nature of their love. The concept of suffering is also key to the impact of this passage. Her hyperbolic assurance that she cares nothing for his sufferings may be taken literally — both Heathcliff and Cathy regularly inflict suffering in ways that suggest they do not care about each other. However, the very act of inflicting suffering is an essential element within their relationship, and as such this sentiment may be seen as an expression of identification and possession.

The nature of their relationship fits in with the Gothic's use of the darker regions of the human spirit; the darkness of the passions of Heathcliff and Cathy and their manifestation is clear to the reader. Their relationship also links to the Gothic form's dependence on the use of opposites and the contradictory, illustrating the importance of the borderlands and limits of the human experience.

Changes in the relationship

The relationship between Cathy and Heathcliff modifies as the novel progresses. It is important to identify its key turning points, and to be able to explain how each affects its development. Below is a list of significant moments in their relationship:

- The visitation of Cathy on the night of Lockwood's stay at the Heights — here the reader sees the extent of Heathcliff's desperation to be reunited with Cathy; we see how far he depends upon her.
- Cathy's 'capture' by the Lintons and her subsequent stay at the Grange — this marks the first major turning point. United in their wild adventure, Heathcliff and Cathy are then separated for the first time. This draws attention to the differences in their social position and the perceived respectability attendant on it. Heathcliff returns to the Heights aware of his inferiority and a barrier begins to erect itself between him and Cathy, aided by the personality of each. Cathy begins her transformation into a 'lady' and becomes increasingly aware of the differences that exist between herself and her childhood companion.
- Cathy's conversation with Nelly, explaining that she cannot marry Heathcliff — Heathcliff, a silent and unseen eavesdropper on their conversation, realises fully

for the first time that he is not good enough for Cathy, who, since her stay at the Grange and her contact with the genteel Edgar, has sensed the division that lies between them. This prompts Heathcliff's disappearance from the locality, an unexplained absence during which he learns to adopt the outward appearance of the gentleman.

- Cathy's marriage to Edgar — in choosing Edgar, Cathy makes it clear that her future does not lie with Heathcliff. This in turn prompts Heathcliff to enter into his 'revenge' marriage with Isabella to hurt both Cathy and Edgar.
- Cathy's illness and madness — this is an essential element in understanding their relationship, as it reawakens Heathcliff's sense of possession and violent love for Cathy.
- Cathy's death — the separation from Cathy's physical body begins Heathcliff's 'haunting' by her spirit; this may be seen as a spiritual extension of the mental 'haunting' that was always a part of their relationship. In terms of his relationship with the other characters in the novel this is also a key moment — Heathcliff becomes increasingly isolated and embittered as his ultimate separation from Cathy begins to take effect.
- Heathcliff's recognition of the similarity of both Hareton and Catherine to his Cathy — this recognition leads to the death of Heathcliff's consuming desire for revenge; he senses a completion and a closure in the budding relationship between the two young people — a completion which he yearns for, but which is denied, as yet, to himself and Cathy. From this point on he seems to prepare himself mentally for his desired reunion with Cathy.
- Heathcliff's death — Cathy and Heathcliff are reunited in their own version of heaven — they are seen to walk together. This suggests that their relationship is still imperfect and uneasy, in that their ghosts have not been laid to rest.

Man and monster

Heathcliff is the dominating figure of the novel. He resembles, but is by no means a straightforward version of, the Byronic hero. Equally, he contains elements of the Gothic villain, albeit an unconventional one. Brontë paints a complex picture of a tormented and tormenting individual. The following section does not exhaust the available textual evidence on Heathcliff, but is intended to provide an overview of some of the more salient areas of his character. The work done here should be supplemented by a detailed gathering of evidence before finally approaching the task of a character study.

Heathcliff is a man of a thousand contradictions: he is a beast, a victim, cruel, capable of the deepest love, a baby, a child, a man, heartless, hateful, affectionate, confident, in need of reassurance, a gentleman, sub-human, superhuman, a Byronic hero, a Machiavellian villain, vengeful and forgiving, sometimes by turns and frequently simultaneously. The reader's perception of him shifts continually. We cannot escape feelings of pity for him, as Nelly and even Edgar admit. However, his behaviour is deplorable and perhaps unforgivable.

No simple summary of a reader's feelings is possible; however, broadly speaking, our sorrow for him at the beginning becomes dislike as the novel progresses, and returns to sympathy as the novel concludes.

Views of Heathcliff

(1) …Mr Heathcliff forms a singular contrast to his abode and style of living. He is a dark-skinned gypsy in aspect, in dress and manners a gentleman — that is, as much a gentleman as many a country squire… (p. 5)

Here Lockwood introduces Heathcliff. He is a man of uncertain and unacceptable parentage and a social misfit (clearly indicated in the denomination of 'gypsy'). Lockwood evidently considers him 'under-bred'. He at once appears as a man of contradictions: he is a gypsy and a gentleman; he provides 'a singular contrast to his abode'.

(2) Heathcliff stood near the entrance, in his shirt and trousers; with a candle dripping over his fingers, and his face as white as the wall behind him. The first creak of the oak startled him like an electric shock: the light leaped from his hold to a distance of some feet, and his agitation was so extreme, that he could hardly pick it up. (p. 26)

Lockwood recounts his encounter with Heathcliff after the visitation of the ghost of Cathy. This passage surprises the reader, as it shows an unexpectedly vulnerable side to Heathcliff — he is capable of shock and extreme emotion.

(3) [Hindley's] treatment of [Heathcliff]…was enough to make a fiend of a saint. And, truly, it appeared as if the lad *were* possessed of something diabolical at that period. He delighted to witness Hindley degrading himself past redemption; and became daily more notable for sullen savageness and ferocity. (p. 66)

This extract emphasises the extent to which Heathcliff may be seen as a victim of circumstances, but without undermining the degree to which he is himself seen as evil. Note the way he takes pleasure in seeing the degradation of Hindley. The reader is aware of Heathcliff's descent into savagery and vengefulness.

(4) A half-civilized ferocity lurked yet in the depressed brows, and eyes full of black fire, but it was subdued; and his manner was even dignified, quite divested of roughness though too stern for grace. (p. 96)

Upon his return from a prolonged and unexplained journey, the reader is forced to note the change that has taken place in Heathcliff; he is no longer presented as some kind of brute, but as something altogether more polished. The air of uncertainty and mystery still lingers about him — nobody knows where he has been — but in the interim he has transformed into a fine, handsome figure of a man, superior in many ways to Mr Linton. However, he is not changed entirely, as he is evidently a passionate, possibly brutal and fiery man; his eyes tell the tale, and now he stands forth as a fearsomely strong and athletic character.

(5) 'He is reformed in every respect, apparently — quite a Christian — offering the right hand of fellowship to his enemies all round!' (p. 99)

The use of the qualifying 'apparently' alerts the reader to the fact that this is merely the calm before the storm. It demonstrates Heathcliff's ability to subdue his violent passions for a short time in order to prepare a foundation for his longer-term plans.

(6) 'Tell her what Heathcliff is — an unreclaimed creature, without refinement — without cultivation; an arid wilderness of furze and whinstone...he's a fierce, pitiless, wolfish man.' (p. 102)

Cathy here encourages Nelly to dissuade Isabella from her romantically idealised views of Heathcliff. The use of wild nature as a comparison for Heathcliff is a good example of Brontë's use of the natural world to reflect the psychological and characteristic states of her characters.

(7) I felt that God had forsaken the stray sheep there to its own wicked wanderings, and an evil beast prowled between it and the fold, waiting his time to spring and destroy. (p. 107)

Nelly here presents Heathcliff as either a sheep under threat or as a satanic beast. This adds to our ambiguous sense of the man — he is not seen as entirely bad, but as a victim, for all his dark evil.

(8) 'Your presence is a moral poison that would contaminate the most virtuous...' (p. 114)

Edgar here portrays Heathcliff as a moral disease. Certainly, he does succeed in contaminating the lives of all those with whom he makes contact, causing his violence and brutality to spread like a plague on to others, as seen in Catherine's maltreatment of Hareton as a result of her maltreatment by Heathcliff. At the same time, however, the reader should be aware that Heathcliff has, at least to some extent, caught this disease himself from the treatment he receives at the hands of Cathy, Hindley and the rest of the Earnshaws.

(9) 'She abandoned them [her family] under a delusion,' he answered, 'picturing in me a hero of romance, and expecting unlimited indulgences from my chivalrous devotion.' (p. 149)

Heathcliff speaks of Isabella's erroneous and unwarranted view of him, and in this identifies what he is not.

(10) 'Don't put faith in a single word he speaks. He's a lying fiend, a monster, and not a human being!' (pp. 150–51)

In this quotation Isabella recognises the essentially untrustworthy and monstrous nature of Heathcliff.

(11) 'I have no pity! I have no pity! The more worms writhe, the more I yearn to crush out their entrails! It is a moral teething, and I grind with greater energy, in proportion to the increase of pain.' (p. 151)

Heathcliff here identifies his own pitiless nature; he sees his consuming anger and cruelty as the result of his own pain; the imagery he employs encourages us to see him as a sadist, in some ways.

(12) 'Poor wretch!' I thought; 'you have a heart and nerves the same as your brother men!' (p. 168)

Nelly, ever a sympathetic narrator, sees in Heathcliff a man at war with himself and the world. This draws the reader's attention to his vulnerability and shows that he is susceptible to human emotion.

(13) '...the casement behind me was banged on to the floor by a blow from [Heathcliff]...and his black countenance looked blightingly through.... His hair and clothes were whitened with snow, and his sharp cannibal teeth, revealed by cold and wrath, gleamed through the dark.' (p. 178)

This extract presents Heathcliff at his most animal-like; he appears as a cannibal seeking to devour his victim. He displays superhuman strength and he 'blights' (infects) the air of the house by his very presence.

(14) '...his basilisk eyes were nearly quenched by sleeplessness — and weeping, perhaps, for the lashes were wet then: his lips devoid of their ferocious sneer, and sealed in an expression of unspeakable sadness. Had it been another, I would have covered my face, in the presence of such grief. (p. 180)

This sums up the contradictory nature of the man. Profound emotion and grief are combined within the 'basilisk' stare. His serpentine and satanic nature is balanced by the deep grief he displays.

(15) 'I don't care for striking, I can't take the trouble to raise my hand! That sounds as if I had been labouring the whole time, only to exhibit a fine trait of magnanimity. It is far from being the case — I have lost the faculty of enjoying their destruction, and I am too idle to destroy for nothing.' (p. 323)

A new and vulnerable side to Heathcliff emerges here. He now displays lethargy and apathy after all his violent, irrepressible energy. The sense of forthcoming change is

impressed upon the reader — the triumph of love over hate, of rebuilding over destruction, of looking to the future instead of brooding on the past.

(16) ...from childhood, he had a delight in dwelling on dark things, and entertaining odd fancies — he might have had a monomania on the subject of his departed idol; but on every other point his wits were as sound as mine. (p. 324)

The 'darkness' of Heathcliff's mind and thoughts is emphasised here, providing an obvious link to the supernatural. Cathy, too, is seen to be interested in the dark areas of spirituality.

(17) '...as to repenting of my injustices, I've done no injustice, and I repent of nothing — I'm too happy, and yet I'm not happy enough. My Soul's bliss kills my body, but does not satisfy itself.' (p. 333)

Heathcliff dies unrepentant, a man full of contradictions he does not even fully understand himself. His lack of penitence makes clear how far removed he is from the realms of conventional Christian religion, but also makes us aware of his profoundly spiritual nature.

Autobiography and fiction

Applying biographical or autobiographical information to a work of fiction, or, indeed, any text, can be both an interesting and an illuminating exercise, although the reader always needs to be very careful when doing so. The following list indicates how the events of Brontë's life find their way into the fictional world of *Wuthering Heights*:

■ The use of isolated locations, so much a part of the life and the passion of Emily Brontë herself, is a central feature in the novel.

■ The brutality of Brontë's school experience is echoed everywhere in the novel; brutality forms a key part of the 'education' of both Heathcliff and Hareton, who are taught their place and deliberately kept in ignorance. There is also a significant difference to draw here between the apparently more educated and refined Lintons and the 'civilised' life at the Grange, and the more brutal and unrefined Heights. Later in the novel, Catherine's caring 'education' of Hareton is essential in restoring peace. Education is thus seen to be a central concern coming out of Brontë's own life.

■ Brontë's strict religious background is mirrored in the religious hypocrisy of Joseph and in Lockwood's dream of the fanatical preacher, Jabes Branderham. Given the strictness of her upbringing, we might be surprised at the dark, irreligious nature of Brontë's tale, or may see in that upbringing the very reason for it.

■ Brontë never enjoyed the experience of travelling from home. Her limited experience of travel (and her lack of desire to do so) is reflected in the limited geographical world of the novel, where the outside world (even nearby Gimmerton) and its representatives are viewed with suspicion. Few characters undertake journeys in the course of the tale, and when they do they are the cause of upheaval.

- The limited family life of the Brontës in their isolated Yorkshire community, and the extent to which they were outsiders, is reflected directly in the claustrophobic world of *Wuthering Heights*.
- The wildness, both of personality and location, which were evidently part of Brontë's childhood, work their way directly into the fictional world of the novel.
- The name Brontë, changed from Brunty, means 'thunder'.
- Family deaths, particularly of young people, form a significant element within both Brontë's life and *Wuthering Heights*.
- The wild male figure of Brontë's brother, the infamous Branwell, is reflected in Heathcliff.
- The absence of a mother figure is significant in both cases, as it is in Gothic literature in general. Mothers do not appear as presences to guide their children; by and large, the guiding role tends to fall into the hands of the male parent.
- In both fact and fiction, for a range of reasons, children are left to face the world alone. This clearly suggests vulnerability and offers an unchecked threat to childhood innocence; this is another common element within Gothic fiction.
- Again, in both fact and fiction, unmarried girls are either left to face the world alone or placed under the protection of ineffective male guardians in a society stacked against them; this, too, is a typical feature of the Gothic genre.
- Emily Brontë's inability to live comfortably as a conventional lady is reflected in the characters of Cathy and Catherine.
- The location of the Brontë family home links to the final image of the novel and its symbolic force (it also links to the important Gothic image of the borderlands).

The role of religion

The use of religion in Gothic fiction is not limited to Christianity alone, although, of course, it is the primary source of references. When approaching any novel within the genre, you need to consider carefully the view of belief that is presented, and the ways in which this affects the views of the reader in each case.

In Gothic works, religion is frequently presented in a far from ideal light. The immoral, unprincipled, often downright evil religious figure is to be found frequently within the pages of these novels (e.g. Ambrosio and the Domina of Saint Claire in *The Monk*) while churches, monasteries and convents, far from being places of refuge, principle and generosity, are places of threat, illegality and self-interest.

This reversal of typical expectations of religion is significant — the Gothic world is a world of reversal, a world where the safe must become unsafe, where the best must be continually threatened by the worst — it is, in short, a form which relies upon the (expectedly) unexpected. Gothic writers play upon the reader's assumption that the good is not as good as it may seem.

By any standards, *Wuthering Heights* is an astonishing novel, especially considering that Emily Brontë was the daughter of a clergyman. It demonstrates a deep awareness of the dark places of the human spirit, exploring in detail the complex and frequently disturbing motivations of a set of characters locked in a cycle of irreligious violence and brutalism. In Heathcliff, Brontë created a character of the profoundest darkness, exploring through him what is arguably the psychology of a psychopath. While operating in conventional religious terms and with established ideas of good and evil, the novel pushes the boundaries of violence and sexuality to the limits (and beyond the limits) of Victorian tolerance.

Examples and analysis

(1)   'Stop, look here, Joseph,' she continued, taking a long dark book from a shelf. 'I'll show you how far I've progressed in the Black Art — I shall soon be competent to make a clear house of it. The red cow didn't die by chance; and your rheumatism can hardly be reckoned among providential visitations!'

'Oh, wicked, wicked!' gasped the elder, 'may the Lord deliver us from evil!'

'No, reprobate! you are a castaway — be off, or I'll hurt you seriously! I'll have you modelled in wax and clay; and the first who passes the limits I fix, shall — I'll not say what he shall be done to — but, you'll see! Go, I'm looking at you!'

The little witch put a mock malignity into her beautiful eyes, and Joseph, trembling with sincere horror, hurried out praying and ejaculating 'wicked' as he went. (p. 15)

This passage focuses significantly upon the dark arts. Joseph connects Catherine with the arcane powers, a situation which she jokingly enjoys. Her attitude is humorously blasphemous. In this the reader sympathises with her to an extent, as Joseph is a religious hypocrite. The introduction of such ideas near the beginning of the novel is important, as the reader later witnesses a sequence of events drawing on bizarre supernatural and arcane powers.

(2)   Another revealing passage is that of Lockwood's dream, from 'I began to dream' to 'to my unspeakable relief, they woke me' (pp. 23–24). This passage records the first of Lockwood's dreams in Volume I, Chapter III, the dream of the 'First of the Seventy First', a sermon delivered by the preacher Jabes Branderham. Coming early in the novel, the focus on the issue of forgiveness of sin is highly significant, as the novel portrays so much sin and so little ability to forgive it; indeed, revenge is the greatest motivating factor within the novel, therefore casting this passage in a highly

ironic light. The concept of transgression (the crossing of boundaries of accept-ability) and trespass is central to the novel, and to the Gothic form. This passage does much to establish an air of nightmarish religious mania in the novel. For the biblical context of this passage, read Matthew 18, verses 21–22.

(3)   Joseph, the servant; you saw him, I dare say, up yonder. He was, and is yet, most likely, the wearisomest, self-righteous pharisee that ever ransacked a Bible to rake the promises to himself, and fling the curses on his neighbours. (p. 42)

Joseph is clearly hypocritical in his religious practice. The reference to the Pharisees is an important one. The Pharisees were Jewish religious teachers renowned for their adherence to the letter rather than the spirit of the law; the adjective 'pharisaical' had worked its way into the English language as early as 1618, referring to those strict in doctrine and ritual, but without the attendant spirit of piety, placing the stress on a superior outward show of morality. The adjective became a byword for hypocrisy, as the Pharisees were regularly referred to by Jesus as hypocrites, and once, famously, as 'you brood of vipers' (Matthew 12, verse 34).

(4)   'I was only going to say that heaven did not seem to be my home; and I broke my heart with weeping to come back to earth; and the angels were so angry that they flung me out, into the middle of the heath on the top of Wuthering Heights....' (p. 81)

Here Cathy speaks of her growing sense of separation from heaven. Wuthering Heights is thus established as a place divorced from heaven, and as such, by definition, may be considered as hell. The novel itself is a world remote from heaven and goodness, and nowhere is the hellish and the evil more in evidence than at the Heights, where brutal violence, hatred and dissent are the norms of existence. This passage develops a particular resonance in view of the subsequent observations of both Cathy and Heathcliff, who seek to establish for themselves a kind of alterna-tive heaven with each other, a heaven which clearly bears little resemblance to the Christian heaven. The reference to being thrown out of heaven establishes connec-tions in the reader's mind with Milton's *Paradise Lost* and the biblical accounts of the fall of Satan and the Fall of humanity.

(5)   'There he has continued, praying like a methodist; only the deity he implored is senseless dust and ashes; and God, when addressed, was curiously confounded with his own black father! After concluding these precious orisons — and they lasted generally till he grew hoarse, and his voice was strangled in his throat — he would be off again...' (p. 175)

Isabella here records Heathcliff's bizarre, satanic and blasphemous prayers of revenge. In many ways this sums up the novel's apparent attitudes towards religion. The reference to the Methodists, a non-conformist sect of Christianity established by the brothers John and Charles Wesley, implies the fervency and dedication of his prayers. The influence of the hellish and the arcane is again clear here.

Brontë also suggests significant connections with two other great literary figures, Lady Macbeth and Frankenstein, both of whom invoke the powers of darkness to aid them in the pursuit of their evil ends, as the following extracts demonstrate:

Lady Macbeth

> Come, you Spirits
> That tend on mortal thoughts, unsex me here,
> And fill me, from the crown to the toe, top-full
> Of direst cruelty! make thick my blood,
> Stop up th'access and passage to remorse;
> That no compunctious visitings of Nature
> Shake my fell purpose, nor keep peace between
> Th'effect and it! Come to my woman's breasts,
> And take my milk for gall, you murd'ring ministers,
> Wherever in your sightless substances
> You wait on Nature's mischief! Come, thick Night,
> And pall thee in the dunnest smoke of Hell,
> That my keen knife see not the wound it makes,
> Nor Heaven peep through the blanket of the dark,
> To cry, 'Hold, hold!'
>
> (*Macbeth*, 1.5.39–53)

Frankenstein

I knelt on the grass, and kissed the earth, and with quivering lips exclaimed, 'By the sacred earth on which I kneel, by the shades that wander near me, by the deep and eternal grief that I feel, I swear; and by thee, O Night, and the spirits that preside over thee, to pursue the daemon, who caused this misery, until he or I shall perish in mortal conflict. For this purpose I will preserve my life: to execute this dear revenge will I again behold the sun, and tread the green herbage of earth, which otherwise should vanish from my eyes forever. And I call on you, spirits of the dead; and on you, wandering ministers of vengeance, to aid and conduct me in my work. Let the cursed and hellish monster drink deep of agony; let him feel the despair that now torments me.'

(*Frankenstein*, p. 206, Penguin 2003)

(6)   'Heathcliff gave [Joseph] a push onto his knees, in the middle of the blood, and flung a towel to him; but instead of proceeding to dry it up, he joined his hands, and began a prayer which excited my laughter from its odd phraseology.' (p. 179)

After Heathcliff has almost killed Earnshaw on his return from a visit to Cathy's grave, Joseph is called in and forced to pray. The prayer, like religion in general, seems oddly out of place in the midst of this violent novel. The image of Joseph on his knees in the middle of a pool of blood provides an apt image for the apparently helpless role of religion. Isabella's laughter at the 'phraseology' of the prayer suggests that religion is misplaced, and how little it is heeded.

(7)   'One might suppose you had never opened a Bible in your life. If God afflict your enemies, surely that ought to suffice you. It is both mean and presumptuous to add your torture to his!' (p. 181)

Nelly Dean speaks to Heathcliff and puts forward the truly Christian view in the face of so much hatred and violence. She appears to be alluding to the biblical principle that vengeance belongs to God and that humans should not seek retribution of their own for wrongs they have suffered (see Romans 12: 19–20).

(8)   'Oh, I owe him so much. On only one condition can I hope to forgive him. It is, if I may take an eye for an eye, a tooth for a tooth, for every wrench of agony, return a wrench, reduce him to my level.' (p. 181)

Isabella, speaking of Heathcliff, invokes the Old Testament maxim of revenge in defence of her position (see Deuteronomy 19: 20–21). This offers a strikingly different perspective to that offered by Nelly Dean in the last example. Isabella has clearly suffered intensely at the hands of her husband, and it is only through the exacting of revenge that she feels her suffering can be atoned for, the balance redressed and forgiveness given. The reader is far from any New Testament concept of forgiveness here (see Matthew 5: 38–42). An interesting comparison is to be drawn with Jabes Branderham's sermon in Lockwood's dream, where he preaches on Christ's doctrine of forgiveness.

(9) Another passage worthy of study is that from '"You are aware, Mr Heathcliff,"' to '"uncoveted by me!"' (p. 333). In this passage we see that conventional religion has no place in Heathcliff's scheme of things. He is fearless and certain in his rejection of Christianity and its demands. Heaven for him is reunion with Cathy — a heaven which has been somewhat hellish in that it seems to have brought him great torment. Even at the last the contradictions remain as Brontë maintains the possibility that for Cathy and Heathcliff an alternative, non-Christian heaven may exist.

Language and religion

Brontë makes use of the language of religion throughout the novel, especially the language of good and evil. The impact of this on the reader is complex. As is clear from the examples above, Brontë's use of religion is far from conventional and straightforward, and the same is true of her use of the language of religion. When we think of religious language we tend to think in terms of moral absolutes, terms which draw meaningful and moral distinctions. The reality of this in *Wuthering Heights*, however, is rather different.

Perhaps the most consistent and striking issue to discuss is the build-up of the language of evil applied to Heathcliff as the novel progresses. He is referred to as 'fiend', 'goblin', 'hellish', 'diabolical', 'evil' and 'demonic', to take but a few examples. Whatever the other differences and disagreements between the characters inhabiting Brontë's fictional world, on the issue of Heathcliff there is at least largely a consensus of opinion. In a novel where the language of religion tends to be used unreliably as a measure of moral judgement, all are in agreement for the majority of the time with regard to him. Equally, the reader should note that, by comparison to Heathcliff, the other characters in general appear to be good, as they so frequently suffer at his hands.

Such a use of stark contrasts of good and evil is reminiscent of the medieval morality plays and is also typical of the oppositions innate within the Gothic form. To see the characters and events of *Wuthering Heights* in such simple terms is, however, misleading. The moral world of this novel is not simply drawn. For all its stark presentation of darkness and evil, the reader needs to remain profoundly aware of the moral relativism of what he/she sees. Characters are frequently seen and described as good or evil in comparison to others; this in itself, however, is no way to value goodness. Instinctively, the reader feels sorrow for the young Heathcliff and the maltreatment he receives at the hands of Hindley (here he appears 'good'). However, such maltreatment cannot ultimately excuse or justify his systematic abuse of other members of the family. Likewise, when he instinctively saves Hareton from death, after Hindley has dropped the child over the banisters, his goodness is immediately undermined by his realisation that he has foiled his own desired revenge on his tormentor.

Similarly, the reader needs at all times to remember the nature of those who are passing moral judgements. Throughout the novel the evaluation of another's goodness or badness is made by characters who are themselves deeply flawed, including Nelly. In the reader's view, therefore, such opinions inevitably become tainted. Joseph's pronouncements on good and evil, for example, cannot be relied upon when his own character is considered. Through her extensive use of the language of good and evil, Brontë achieves a strangely disconcerting effect; conceptions of good and evil are strangely transmogrified and lose the ability to act as a moral absolute.

Location and journeys

Initial bearings

From the beginning, *Wuthering Heights* places an important emphasis upon location. The title of the novel is, in itself, an indication of the significance of place in the fictional world the reader is about to enter. Without delay, he/she is introduced, by Lockwood, to the wilderness of the Yorkshire moors and the even wilder Wuthering Heights and its inhabitants. The role of journeys is also essential as the novel opens; Lockwood has journeyed from the south to take up tenancy of Thrushcross Grange.

Although this may seem insignificant at first, the reader soon becomes aware of the profoundly insular world of the Yorkshire moors and in particular the claustrophobia of the communities of the Grange and the Heights. In the face of the largely static nature of so many of the novel's events (which seem to rotate in a vicious circle of repetition within and across generations), Lockwood's travels are something exceptional. He is at once (and brutally) established as an outsider and a 'foreigner' — an onlooker, like the reader.

Brontë's purposes in this are pivotal to appreciating her novel. In focusing our attention narrowly on the world of the Heights and its rugged wildness, Brontë prepares us from the outset for the claustrophobia and inescapable violence that is so central to the tale. The very lack of travel in the course of the novel emphasises the impossibility of escape for the characters from the excess and the brutality they face on an almost daily basis. Equally, the lack of visitors and passers-by adds to the disturbing and threatening isolation of the characters within their violent milieu. The prospects of escape or rescue are clearly limited.

To the ends of the Earth

The novel begins with a framing narrative. Lockwood, the frame narrator, is isolated in an unfamiliar and largely unwelcoming society, far from home and family. He is not an intrepid man, and is engaged on a journey of pleasure, looking for a peaceful retreat. This reflects his social position as a member of the leisured gentry. His travels, however, are destined to bring him anything but the peace and pleasure he desires. Instead, he finds himself in a place that may very well be described as the ends of the earth. Once he arrives on the moors, Brontë establishes without delay the relationship between Lockwood and his immediate counterpart, Heathcliff. This is a telling comparison as the novel develops: both men are (technically at least) gentlemen, and both experience the extreme difficulties of arriving as an outsider within the social circle of the Heights and the Grange. Lockwood is clearly alert to the similarities and the differences between himself and Heathcliff, when he observes, 'Mr Heathcliff and I are such a suitable pair to divide the desolation between us' (p. 3).

Throughout the novel the physical journey is closely connected to the spiritual and psychological journeys the characters are engaged upon. The journeys of knowledge and experience and the physical journey are inextricably linked. Lockwood and Heathcliff arrive in Yorkshire as outsiders and, having ended the physical journey, begin a new and far more demanding voyage of self-discovery.

Apart from a few exceptional long journeys, movement within the text occurs within the limited locale of the Grange, the Heights and Gimmerton, the nearest village; and even this place, 4 miles distant from the Heights and almost 8 miles from the Grange, appears to be a whole world away from the loneliness of life in either of the houses. The majority of the traffic in the novel is between the Heights and the Grange, which serves to highlight further the inescapable forces that seem to encircle and bind these places and their inhabitants. Brontë uses the very lack of movement in her tale to intensify the dangers apparent from within the communities of the Heights and the Grange.

Brontë is concerned not only with the fact of the journey (or lack of journey), but also with where this leads; in this case the inhospitable, yet curiously beautiful moorland landscape of Yorkshire. The reader is presented not simply with an untamed Gothic landscape, but with a location that reflects the very nature of the tale recounted. The physical threats posed by the harsh weather and punishing conditions of life in the wilds of the moors encapsulate the brutal, strange and harrowing stories Brontë unfolds. As Lockwood early on informs the reader, the name of Wuthering Heights is in itself portentous, '"Wuthering" being a significant provincial adjective, descriptive of the atmospheric tumult to which its station is exposed in stormy weather' (p. 4). The location of the house is thus seen to impose upon its inhabitants a symbolic weight of disturbance, discord and harshness. The blizzard that opens *Wuthering Heights* becomes the embodiment of the mad obsessions and the encroaching dangers that face Lockwood in his new abode. The extreme nature of the story depends, for its success, upon the willingness of the reader to operate at the utmost limits of experience and plausibility, and this extremity is embodied in the settings. As is the case with *Frankenstein*, *Dracula* and other texts in the Gothic tradition, the very ruggedness and wildness of the location acts as a curious verification or guarantee of events that may otherwise be dismissed as mere fantasy.

In dealing with the extremes of human nature, and in considering the lengths to which human beings will allow themselves to be pushed by their unquenchable desire for knowledge or revenge, Brontë's use of untamed locations is central. The landscapes presented to the reader become a metaphor for the rugged harshness and uncontrollable wildness to which single-minded, irresponsible determination can lead. They become the fearsome frontiers of human intellect and passion.

The mountains of the mind

The use of location and landscape to reflect the human psyche is central here. The untamed wilderness of the moors, simultaneously a place of the greatest natural beauty and the greatest natural threat, represents the spiritual wilderness that is the mental reality of so many of the characters in the novel. The rapid and violent dislocations of their lives are mirrored in the seasonal changes and the climatic conditions of the moors themselves. The radically differing natures of the moors is highly important in shedding light on the relationship between Heathcliff and Cathy, where love and hate, comfort and pain, unity and division vie openly with one another. The almost insane passion demonstrated by both characters, and their faith in the spiritual and the existence of the ghost-world, is reflected in the shifting lights and seasons of the moors. Faced with the ineradicable need to confront their obsessions, they become, in burial, a part of the spiritual wastelands they inhabited. Other key examples of this are found in the blizzard that forces Lockwood to spend a nightmarish night at the Heights, which is a symbol of spiritual and moral imprisonment, and the unforgettable storm that marks the departure of Heathcliff from the Grange.

The desolate moors

The disturbing impact of Brontë's tale is heightened by the contrast she draws between 'civilised', controlled nature (as represented in the garden and the park) and the wilderness of the moors. The inhospitable moors provide a fitting backdrop to the events of the novel, reflecting the harsh and difficult nature of life and the Heights and the Grange. In their isolated location, distanced from the nearest 'civilisation' at Gimmerton, the Grange and the Heights are cut off from normality and the restriction of societal expectation and codes. The characters are vulnerable to maltreatment by those who live around them; this is reflected in the extent to which the characters find themselves at the mercy of nature and the elements. Lockwood's opening description of the Heights is an excellent example of this. The bleakness of the moors, coupled with the violent shifts in weather that take place, demonstrate the turbulent nature of life within the Linton and Earnshaw households. Similarly, when in the concluding pages of the novel Lockwood draws attention to the radical differences seen in the Yorkshire landscape from season to season, he encapsulates both the beauty and the hideousness of human nature.

The conclusion of *Wuthering Heights* is markedly ambiguous in its views of isolation. The wildness and loneliness of the author's beloved native landscape is both its salvation and its damnation, a fact that links profoundly to the lives and experiences of the characters of the novel. If, on one hand, the novel offers fulfilment in the conventional union of Catherine and Hareton, with all its promise of new life and a new start, it also offers an alternative and radically unconventional union in the final restoration of Heathcliff to Cathy. For all that Cathy haunts him over the 18 years after her death, the end of the novel effects a bizarre reconciliation, though whether this will lead to final happiness in an alternative 'heaven', or torment in an eternal 'hell', is left uncertain. The moors remain a potent symbol of these two relationships.

The journey of the narrative

Given the significance of location and journey in the text, it is important to consider the structural 'journey' that Brontë employs, too. *Wuthering Heights* traces a set of journeys. Lockwood's journey to the north and his resulting contact with the almost other-worldly events at the Heights and the Grange takes him to the dark heart of human nature, a place which he then leaves, but to which he significantly returns at the end of the tale, providing a satisfying, cyclical conclusion. The structural interdependency of the various narratives, filtered through the centralising consciousness of Nelly Dean, provides a forceful logic to the tale. Nelly's unique perspective allows her to map the 'journey' of the two houses, as the Earnshaws and the Lintons are gradually drawn together by the forces of intermarriage and time.

The journey ends fittingly with a vision of three graves. The reader and Lockwood face the tombs of Edgar, Cathy and Heathcliff on the boundary of the churchyard and the moor. The setting of this final scene is highly suggestive — we are on the borders of the tame and the wild, the holy and the unholy, the dead and the living, the lover and the beloved, the elevated and the earthly, the spiritual and the bodily. It has been a journey from life to death, but also from death to life; from love to hate, but also from hate to love. Brontë's narrative has been a journey of ambiguity, which is reflected in this final choice of location.

Isolation and outsiders

The outsider is a key figure in the Gothic novel. Living beyond the bounds of conventional society or on the borderlands of it, he or she is seen as a suspicious and threatening entity, someone who must be excluded for the safety of society at large. Key figures of the Gothic imagination such as Frankenstein, his monster, Count Dracula, the Ancient Mariner and the Wandering Jew have all now taken their place in mainstream culture. They are examples of how the outsider becomes the enemy, the threat to decent society and morality, and yet also occupies a position of vulnerability. The Gothic explores this at great length; Count Dracula not only victimises the virginal women of Victorian society, threatening to undermine the social institution of marriage, but is himself plagued and victimised by society at large. Similarly, but more sympathetically in the reader's eyes, Heathcliff in *Wuthering Heights* not only commits acts of aggression, but is himself on the receiving end of much unwarranted cruelty.

Lastly we must consider in this context the innocent victims of evil and darkness in the Gothic novel, the men, women and children who, for a variety of reasons, find themselves unable to fulfil the (often unreasonable) demands placed upon them by tyrannical authorities or authority figures, and are therefore punished.

Isolation is a concept within the Gothic closely linked to the idea of the outsider. Many of the outsiders of Gothic fiction find themselves isolated, both literally and metaphorically. Think of the isolated castles of the romances of Ann Radcliffe, Castle Dracula deep in the Carpathian Mountains, the Woman in Black on the Eel Marsh, and Frankenstein and his monster on the mountain-tops or in the far reaches of the Arctic. The distance of these locations from the safety of conventional society emphasises the threat posed simultaneously by and to the people who dwell there.

Almost all the characters in *Wuthering Heights* can be considered in the light of this issue at some point in the novel. Even within the tight-knit family circles of the Lintons and the Earnshaws, people easily fall into disfavour or otherwise alienate themselves from their families and neighbours. Part of the problem is the extreme isolation (spiritual, physical and mental) faced by the inhabitants of Brontë's world. Although they are forever surrounded by the members of their family, many of the characters suffer an increasing sense of loss and loneliness, unable as they are to develop meaningful, loving and trusting relationships. All that remains for them is the dream of a perfect companionship. This is strikingly evident in the dreams of Cathy and Heathcliff, and also in Isabella's self-delusion and fantasy in casting Heathcliff as a Byronic romantic hero. In both cases, any hope of a conventional 'dream' relationship is quickly dispelled and shattered. Almost without exception, the inhabitants of the Heights and the Grange find themselves reduced from positions of domestic security to cloying isolation. All of the characters (even Heathcliff) display a desperate need for meaningful and reliable companionship. The love and devotion felt for Nelly Dean, in the absence of any lasting maternal figure, is clear evidence of this. The various marriages of the book are surely proof of a continued yearning for fulfilment and unity; however, with the final exception of the union between Catherine and Hareton, they are not about companionship so much as confrontation, sources not of comfort and kindness but of further pain and brutality. Isolation is a reality the characters find themselves incapable of escaping.

The concept of physical and spiritual isolation is of considerable importance in the novel; however, the narrative line of the tale can be seen as a process of movement from separation and dislocation towards unity. The whole process is complicated by outsiders, such as Heathcliff and Linton, who serve to poison an already difficult and tainted atmosphere. The Grange and the Heights are isolated from one another, but at the same time are integrally linked to one another — there seems to be some kind of spiritual affinity between them, as there is between Heathcliff and Cathy.

The novel is also a study in the psychological and social impact of isolation and cruelty, looking at the ways in which it can affect the individual, the family and society at large. Although *Wuthering Heights* takes place in a microcosm, its messages and impact are universal.

Examples and analysis

(1) In all England, I do not believe that I could have fixed on a situation so completely removed from the stir of society. (p. 3)

Lockwood's observation at the beginning of the novel indicates the extent to which Wuthering Heights stands alone and isolated. This is clearly symbolic, distancing the cruel, barbarous and bizarrely excessive events of the text from the everyday world of the reader; it also emphasises the defencelessness of the novel's victims, who are kept far from any external source of aid. The loneliness of the situation makes it inevitable that Lockwood, as a newcomer, will be perceived as an interloper, an outsider.

(2) We don't in general take to foreigners here, Mr Lockwood, unless they take to us first. (p. 46)

Nelly Dean speaks of Hindley's wife, Frances, but emphasises the difficulties faced by Heathcliff, Linton and Lockwood as well, all of whom have to try to fit into the social world of the Heights and the Grange.

(3) '…he is that strange acquisition my late neighbour made in his journey to Liverpool — a little Lascar, or an American or Spanish castaway.' (p. 50)

This is Mr Linton's view of Heathcliff. His comments demonstrate the dismissive attitude of the neighbourhood towards 'foreigners' and outsiders.

(4) '…living among the hills, and seeing one set of faces, and one series of actions, from year's end to year's end…' (p. 63)

Nelly here describes life on the moors. She emphasises the isolation and the social claustrophobia of life in *Wuthering Heights*. The atmosphere in which the characters live adds to the novel's sense of inescapable danger and violence. This quotation adds to the sense of inevitability in the novel, too, as if from one year to the next events are destined to stay the same and the cycle of domestic violence and mental cruelty is bound to continue.

(5) I could not half tell what an infernal house we had. The curate dropped calling, and nobody decent came near us, at last… (p. 66)

Nelly Dean, speaking of life after the death of Mrs Earnshaw, demonstrates the extent to which the family has become isolated and shunned even by local society. The novel operates in a very narrow world.

(6) 'But, supposing at twelve years old, I had been wrenched from the Heights, and every early association, and my all in all, as Heathcliff was at that time, and been converted at a stroke into Mrs Linton, the lady of Thrushcross Grange, and the wife of a stranger; an exile, and outcast, thenceforth, from what had been my world — You may fancy a glimpse of the abyss where I grovelled!' (p. 125)

Cathy here describes her situation (and that of Heathcliff) after her marriage to Edgar Linton. Note the imagery of isolation and the abyss she employs.

(7) 'You'll not be surprised, Ellen, at my feeling particularly cheerless, seated in worse than solitude, on that inhospitable hearth, and remembering that four miles distant lay my delightful home, containing the only people I loved on earth: and there might as well be the Atlantic to part us, instead of those four miles, I could not overpass them!' (pp. 138–39)

Isabella comments on her life at Wuthering Heights after her marriage to Heathcliff. The 4 miles which separate her from her family at the Grange seem insurmountable, illustrating the danger of her position. This also emphasises the rift between Isabella and her brother, Edgar, after her marriage to Heathcliff.

(8)   The place of Catherine's interment, to the surprise of the villagers, was neither in the chapel, under the carved monument of the Lintons, nor yet by the tombs of her own relations, outside. It was dug on a green slope, in a corner of the kirkyard, where the wall is so low that heath and bilberry plants have climbed over it from the moor; and peat mould almost buries it. (p. 170)

Note the location of Cathy's grave. This indicates the extent to which she is separated from the rest of her family and from the society of Gimmerton. It is a spot isolated within the churchyard and reclaimed by the wildness of the moor, as befits her nature.

(9)   Till she reached the age of thirteen, she had not once been beyond the range of the park by herself. Mr Linton would take her with him, a mile or so outside, on rare occasions; but he trusted her to no one else. Gimmerton was an unsubstantial name in her ears, the chapel, the only building she had approached, or entered, except her own home; Wuthering Heights and Mr Heathcliff did not exist for her; she was a perfect recluse; and, apparently, perfectly contented. (p. 190)

Catherine is kept isolated by her father, Edgar Linton, as part of his efforts to protect her. Compare and contrast this to the imprisonment and isolation others suffer in the novel.

(10)   'Mr Heathcliff, *you* have *nobody* to love you; and, however miserable you make us, we shall still have the revenge of thinking that your cruelty rises from your greater misery! You *are* miserable, are you not? Lonely, like the devil, and envious like him? *Nobody* loves you — *nobody* will cry for you, when you die! I wouldn't be you!' (p. 288)

Catherine speaks to Heathcliff, emphasising the extent to which he is isolated within the text. Almost universally rejected, Heathcliff is, arguably, the most helplessly alienated of all the characters in the novel, and as a result he determines to inflict on others the isolation from which he has suffered, by way of revenge.

Themes and imagery

The elements

In a novel that deals with power and raw, elemental emotion, it is not surprising that Brontë makes extensive use of the imagery of the elements. The power of the natural world is an apt representation of the characters and their shifting emotions as the novel progresses, often appearing as an externalisation of those emotions and their potential.

Significant in this context is the notion of the four temperaments or 'humours' said to be found in each individual. Blood, phlegm, choler (anger) and melancholy (or black choler) are linked to the elements of earth, air, fire and water. The ideal temperament was believed to be one which contained all four of these humours in equal measure, while the preponderance of any one of them led to an imbalance and a consequent failing in character. This adds an intriguing dimension to the use Brontë makes of the elements, especially in her deployment of elemental pathetic fallacy to create atmosphere. The most striking use occurs at moments in the novel where rationality and balance are least in evidence, and Brontë uses them directly and sometimes ironically to achieve her impact on the reader.

The elements are a central part of the nature that Brontë loved so deeply — she could never bear to be parted from her beloved moorland home for long, although it was a harsh and inhospitable place at times. Throughout the novel, Brontë makes considerable use of the moors and the elements to convey meaning, to create mood or atmosphere, and to reflect the mental state of her characters (see also the comparisons between *Wuthering Heights* and *King Lear* on pages 19–21). In the following short passages, Brontë makes considerable use of the elements to create strikingly different effects. You need to be able to explain, with close reference to the language she uses, both the effects she achieves and the way she achieves them.

The first passage occurs shortly after Heathcliff has run away from the Heights, having heard that Cathy is to marry Edgar (pp. 84–85).

> It *was* a very dark evening for summer: the clouds appeared inclined to thunder, and I said we had better all sit down, the approaching rain would be certain to bring him home without further trouble.
>
> However, Catherine would not be persuaded into tranquillity. She kept wandering to and fro, from the gate to the door, in a state of agitation which permitted no repose, and at length took up a permanent situation on one side of the wall, near the road; where, heedless of my expostulations, and the growling thunder, and the great drops that began to plash around her, she remained, calling at intervals, and then listening, and then crying outright. She beat Hareton, or any child, at a good, passionate fit of crying.
>
> About midnight, while we still sat up, the storm came rattling over the Heights in full fury. There was a violent wind, as well as thunder, and either one or the other split a tree off the corner of the building; a huge bough fell across the roof, and knocked down a portion of the east chimney-stack, sending a clatter of stones and soot into the kitchen fire.

Here Brontë uses the storm to reflect a wide range of issues within the novel. It may be taken to:

■ represent the separation of Cathy and Heathcliff and the intense emotion this evokes in both of them

■ symbolise the personal and spiritual turmoil and upset to which their ambiguous relationship leads

- represent the dislocation and division both within and between the families of Earnshaw and Linton
- symbolise the relationship of Cathy and Heathcliff
- embody the anger of Heathcliff which is to be unleashed against the inhabitants of the Heights as a result of what has just taken place
- be a symbolic presentation of the madness of the characters — as when Nelly recalls Cathy's reaction to the disappearance of Heathcliff: '…I shall never forget what a scene she acted, when we reached her chamber. It terrified me — I thought she was going mad, and I begged Joseph to run for the doctor' (p. 88).

The second passage to consider is that where Nelly Dean is out in the garden on the night that Heathcliff returns to Yorkshire (p. 93).

> On a mellow evening in September, I was coming from the garden with a heavy basket of apples which I had been gathering. It had got dusk, and the moon looked over the high wall of the court, causing undefined shadows to lurk in the corners of the numerous projecting portions of the building. I set my burden on the house steps by the kitchen door, and lingered to rest, and draw in a few more breaths of the soft, sweet air; my eyes were on the moon, and my back to the entrance, when I heard a voice behind me say —
>
> 'Nelly, is that you?'

Brontë's use of the elements to create an ambiguously misleading atmosphere is striking. The pleasant natural description of the early autumn evening is given a faintly threatening tinge by the presence of the 'undefined shadows' which prefigure the undefined man who awaits Nelly's return, a prelude not to autumnal fruitfulness, comfort and pleasure, but rather to fear. Brontë uses the weather to prepare for and to contrast the emotions and atmosphere of Heathcliff's return. The fine weather and the 'soft, sweet air' are soon to be lost in the blast of winter, as the peace of the Heights and the Grange is to be blasted by Heathcliff's anger.

Violence

Violence, be it actual, imagined or verbal, is the norm. Almost without exception, the characters of *Wuthering Heights* indulge in acts of gratuitous brutality. Unusually, this violence does not remain the preserve of the male characters. Brontë's presentation of violence encompasses a wide range of aspects, including love, frustration, revenge, isolation, and at times even black humour.

Violence and brutality permeate every aspect of the work. Cathy and Heathcliff's relationship is marked throughout by its violent passions and equally violent rows. Their meetings often appear more animal-like than human. The relationships between Heathcliff and Isabella and Heathcliff and Catherine are likewise characterised by harshness and cruelty and even lack any redeeming passion. Isabella's elopement with Heathcliff is signalled with the hanging of the dog, and ends with a murderous attempt on her life. In trying to protect the young Hareton from his drunken father, Nelly Dean is made to 'eat' Hindley's knife, and Catherine expresses her frustration at her imprisonment at the Heights through vituperative words and physical violence against Hareton and Heathcliff.

Such ubiquitous violence has a profound effect upon the reader, and it necessitates a steady escalation of brutality as the text advances; otherwise it loses the power to shock. This can be seen to have an impact, too, upon the mentality of the characters, all of whom develop an immunity to the acts of horror they see enacted around them every day, and enter into a pact of silence as their perceptions harden. The prevalence of such violence creates the permanent sense of threat that exists in the novel; it suggests the presence of social disorder and the dysfunction of the households of Earnshaw and Linton. The failure of conventional communication means that words no longer have the power to heal, but seem only to aggravate the characters further, until at last Catherine is able to teach Hareton and herself a new language, a language of reconciliation and love, as he literally learns language under her tuition.

The abyss and the mountain

The abyss and the mountain are highly significant images in Gothic fiction. For obvious physical reasons they are generally taken (along with other images such as towers, spires, caverns, pits, cellars and so on) to be representations of the feminine and the masculine respectively. Mountains and other linked images are taken as representations of the phallus, symbolising thrusting male activity and dominance, whilst the dark caverns and their vaginal counterparts are seen to symbolise feminine passivity and weakness. This has implications for a Freudian reading of these texts, which relies heavily on the hidden (sometimes only thinly veiled) sexual motivations for action and inaction.

Both the abyss and the mountain have significant religious overtones too. The abyss is an image of hell and damnation. The book of Revelation, among others, refers to the abyss into which Satan or the Beast is cast, and from which he will emerge as the Antichrist to unleash 1,000 years of terror on the earth before the return of Christ at the Second Coming (see Revelation 20). This reading works quite differently to the Freudian interpretation, in that the dark places, the caverns and the abyss become places of dark power, the source not of passivity but of active evil and lurking threat. The mountain is also a significant biblical image; consider the use of mountains as holy places in biblical stories such as that of Noah, when the Ark lands on the heights of Mount Ararat (Genesis 8: 1–5), the giving of the Law to Moses on Mount Sinai (Exodus 19 and 20), the defeat of the prophets of Baal by Elijah on Mount Carmel (1 Kings 18), the story of the Transfiguration (Matthew 17: 1–13), the famous Sermon on the Mount (Matthew 5 onwards), and the temptation of Christ on the mountain by Satan (Matthew 4: 1–11). In all of these stories the mountain is presented as a place of holiness and power through divine revelation.

In *Wuthering Heights*, Brontë makes use of two 'high' locations. Unbeknown to her father and Nelly, Catherine undertakes a journey to Penistone Crags. It is on this journey that she first encounters Heathcliff. The dominating physical presence of the Crags seems to act as a powerful lure to the inexperienced young Catherine, attracting her to what will prove to be a destructive relationship with both Linton and Heathcliff. The Heights, as its name makes clear, is a 'high' location too, and as such contrasts to the relatively low-lying Thrushcross Grange. As the novel progresses, the Heights is increasingly taken as a symbol of aggressive male power, while the Grange comes to be a symbol of feminine passivity. This is also significant in relation to a biblical interpretation, as both Penistone Crags and the Heights prove to be places of revelation, places where characters find enlightenment, albeit an enlightenment that has distinctly dark overtones.

Sanity/insanity

The boundary between sanity and insanity is explored frequently in Gothic literature, and plays an important part in *Wuthering Heights*. It links closely to the concept of the borderlands. Much of what the reader encounters in the novel seems to be insane:

- Heathcliff and Cathy demonstrate the great and profoundly disturbing power of a love that may be seen as madness
- a number of characters make what seem to be insane choices, as when Isabella, in the face of a blunt warning from Cathy, insists on eloping with Heathcliff
- the novel repeatedly makes use of frenzied violence — mindless brutality is almost the norm in this world of inverted values
- Cathy and Heathcliff, in particular, seem to dwell on the very cusp of madness, as Nelly observes on a number of occasions

It is frequently unclear whether sanity or insanity prevails, and the terms become almost meaningless in helping the reader to make moral or human judgements, as the absolutes implied by the terms 'sane' and 'insane' cease to exist. Brontë's vocabulary, e.g. 'frenzy', 'ecstasy', 'fit of passion' and 'delirium', clouds the issue further.

Death

Death is never far off in the novel. Cathy, Frances, Isabella, Linton and Heathcliff (who, while not particularly young, is, as Lockwood points out, very fit and healthy) die young, though surprisingly not as a result of the ubiquitous physical violence, even where it takes deadly forms. Threats of death and murder are to be found throughout the novel; they are part and parcel of life at the Heights.

Again, the reader needs to be aware of the symbolic importance of these images. Through his relentless pursuit of revenge and violence, Heathcliff unleashes a dreadful threat on the world. This emphasises the fragility of human existence in the fictional world of the text. It is also important to note that moral death and destruction is suggested by the physical death and destruction that constantly threatens to engulf the novel. There is a pathetic redundancy in the readiness with which many of the characters resort to their threats of violence and annihilation.

The powerful final image of the novel is of the graveyard and specifically the three graves of Cathy, Edgar and Heathcliff; this emphasises the significance that death has had within the novel, but equally undermines it. The reader readily remembers that death in this novel is not always a binding force. Cathy has 'walked' for 18 years, during which she has continued to visit and torment Heathcliff, and the implication is clear that they walk again as a couple, reunited in death.

Blood

Blood is a central image within the text. It develops a set of powerful overtones as the novel progresses. In key Gothic texts such as *Dracula* and *Frankenstein*, blood and sexual fluids become, at times, almost interchangeable. Blood also becomes linked to sex and sexual excess in *Wuthering Heights*. A particularly striking example is the occasion upon which Heathcliff, having visited Cathy's grave, returns to the Heights and nearly kills Hareton, and then forces Joseph to kneel in the midst of the pool of blood. The letting of blood here symbolises the pent-up sexual frustration of Heathcliff's relationship with Cathy. There are repeated examples of blood being shed, and it takes on an almost ritual significance as the novel progresses. In addition, the repeated emphasis on blood is connected in the reader's mind to the concept of revenge.

The image of blood also develops considerable importance in terms of blood-relationship and blood-lines in the novel. *Wuthering Heights* traces the coming together of two houses. The mingling of Earnshaw and Linton blood is highly significant, especially in terms of Heathcliff's claims upon Thrushcross Grange. It is with the marriage of Catherine and Hareton that union is finally achieved — both of blood and of purpose.

The supernatural

Throughout *Wuthering Heights*, Emily Brontë makes use of the supernatural. As in *Frankenstein*, where Shelley uses this technique in an unusual way, Brontë's deployment of the device is unconventional. Like the monster in Shelley's novel, Heathcliff is not supernatural in the sense that he is paranormal, but in that he appears superhuman — bigger, stronger and in every way larger than the world around him. A large part of the fearsome power of Brontë's tale lies in the fact that Heathcliff is flesh and blood — the horror and brutality of his actions may make him seem supernatural, but the reader and the other characters are not given the comfort, until the very end, of removing him to the realms of the other world. Strikingly, however, this is the way that Brontë and her narrators frequently seek to present him — he is by turns referred to as a 'vampire' and a 'goblin', and Linton perceives his father as a malevolent spirit looking down on his meetings with Catherine from the Heights. The novel therefore deviates from the conventional supernatural found in *The Castle of Otranto*, *The Monk*, *Melmoth the Wanderer* and other great Gothic novels. Nor does it adhere to the explained supernatural technique favoured by Ann Radcliffe, where occurrences that have throughout the novel appeared to be supernatural are given a rational explanation at last. The fear of the reader of *Wuthering Heights* is the inescapable reality of Heathcliff.

The relationship between the natural and the supernatural in Brontë's presentation of Heathcliff is complex. The blurring of the boundaries between the two is key here — Brontë repeatedly causes her reader to question where the border lies. The waters are muddied further by the incursion of the *un*natural and the *preter*-natural (alongside the natural and the supernatural) into the reader's view of this highly complex and fascinating man.

Fear of Heathcliff is engendered constantly through the deep uncertainty the reader and the other characters feel in response to him. In this tale, where so much that is unnatural (Heathcliff's insatiable, passionate and extraordinarily violent revenge) and preternatural (Heathcliff consistently demonstrates a heightened awareness, almost to the point of prescience, of the events surrounding him) occurs, the transfer to the world of the *super*natural is often made. The natural and supernatural worlds are seen to coexist and to impinge on each other frequently.

In the lives of Cathy and Heathcliff the supernatural plays a significant role, even in childhood, when they call up the ghosts in the graveyard of Gimmerton Kirk. After Cathy's death this continues, Heathcliff living in such a heightened state of awareness of the supernatural that he almost becomes part of the supernatural world himself. The natural relationship between Cathy and Heathcliff can only take place in the terms of (and actually in) the supernatural world.

At the same time, however, the reader is constantly made aware, through the eyes of Nelly Dean, that Heathcliff is a man of flesh and blood. He is capable of feelings and emotions, of bleeding and dying like those around him. The cruel neglect and maltreatment he suffers at the hands of Hindley after the death of old Mr Earnshaw, his protector, earns Heathcliff some measure of the reader's sympathy. Likewise, the reader feels his pain as he overhears the fateful conversation between Nelly and Cathy, from which he learns that he can never be Cathy's husband. Brontë is always careful to ensure that the reader sees in Heathcliff a balance of the good and the bad, reflected in a complex interweaving of the natural and the supernatural.

Elements of the Gothic supernatural are also present in the reactions of the characters to Heathcliff. Although he is a creature of flesh and blood with, as Brontë is frequently at pains to point out, genuine human emotions, Heathcliff nonetheless evokes in all who see him reactions as if he were a ghost. As a stalking presence, watching from his vantage point at the Heights, he shares many ghost-like qualities, and can be compared to other great wandering figures of the Gothic, such as the Wandering Jew and Count Dracula.

The visitations of the ghosts of Cathy and Heathcliff in the course of the novel represent a more conventional deployment of the supernatural.

Examples and analysis

Below is a selection of passages in which Brontë makes use of the supernatural. For each example it is essential to explore and explain in detail its significance and the impact it has upon the reader.

(1) The sun shone yellow on its grey head, reminding me of summer; and I cannot say why, but all at once, a gush of child's sensations flowed into my heart. Hindley and I held it a favourite spot twenty years before.

I gazed long at the weather-worn block; and, stooping down, perceived a hole near the bottom still full of snail-shells and pebbles which we were fond of storing there with more perishable things — and, as fresh as reality, it appeared that I beheld my early playmate seated on the withered turf; his dark, square head bent forward, and his little hand scooping out the earth with a piece of slate.

'Poor Hindley!' I exclaimed, involuntarily.

I started — my bodily eye was cheated into a momentary belief that the child lifted its face and stared straight into mine! It vanished in a twinkling; but, immediately, I felt an irresistible yearning to be at the Heights. Superstition urged me to comply with this impulse — supposing he should be dead! I thought — or should die soon! — supposing it were a sign of death!

The nearer I got to the house the more agitated I grew; and on catching sight of it, I trembled every limb. The apparition had outstripped me; it stood looking through the gate. That was my first idea on observing an elf-locked, brown-eyed boy setting his ruddy countenance against the bars. Further reflection suggested this must be Hareton, *my* Hareton, not altered greatly since I left him, ten months since. (pp. 108–09)

Note the power of superstition and the supernatural here. Nelly finds her actions dictated by some greater, irresistible power, under the influence of which she finds herself compelled to hurry to the Heights. Note too the phantasmagoric merging of the real and the supernatural in the ghost of Hindley and the reality of Hareton; at the end of the passage the reader is granted no certainty as to what Nelly has in fact seen. This adds to the novel's often confusing doubling of characters, and contributes to its sense of timeless claustrophobia, as Nelly leaps backwards and forwards across the time of the story in her mind.

(2)   'It's a rough journey, and a sad heart to travel it; and we must pass by Gimmerton Kirk, to
       go that journey! We've braved its ghosts often together, and dared each other to stand
       among the graves and ask them to come…But Heathcliff, if I dare you now, will you
       venture? If you do, I'll keep you. I'll not lie there by myself; they may bury me twelve feet
       deep, and throw the church down over me; but I won't rest till you are with me…I never
       will!' (p. 126)

This passage invokes the supernatural element of the relationship between Heathcliff
and Cathy. It has already been introduced by the visitation of Cathy's ghost in
Lockwood's nightmare. The way is prepared for Heathcliff's digging up of Cathy's
grave, and for the later sightings of Heathcliff and Cathy once they have been
reunited in death. Furthermore, it links Heathcliff and Cathy firmly to the supernatural in their calling on the ghosts; it is as if the natural world is not capable of
dealing with such extremes of passion.

(3)   'Last night, I was in the Grange garden six hours, and I'll return there to-night; and every
       night I'll haunt the place, and every day, till I find an opportunity of entering.' (p. 151)

Heathcliff presents himself as a determined, tormenting spirit. Brontë frequently
uses such language in order to create the impression that Heathcliff is a supernatural power within the world of the novel. Compare this image to the visitation
of the spirit of Catherine Linton, yearning for admittance to the Heights in
Lockwood's nightmare.

(4)   '…my presence is as potent on his nerves, as a ghost; and I fancy he sees me often, though I
       am not near. Hareton says he wakes and shrieks in the night by the hour together; and calls
       you to protect him from me…' (p. 287)

Heathcliff speaks of his influence over his son, Linton. Notice the language he
deploys, describing himself as a spiritual presence of fear watching over Linton. A
similar effect is evident in the scenes where Catherine and Nelly ride out to meet
Linton prior to his marriage to Catherine. Linton's reactions suggest Heathcliff's
overwatching presence, driving him towards wedlock with Catherine.

(5)   '…I gave some ease to myself. I shall be a great deal more comfortable now; and you'll have
       a better chance of keeping me underground, when I get there. Disturbed her? No! she has
       disturbed me, night and day, through eighteen years — incessantly — remorselessly — till
       yesternight — and yesternight, I was tranquil. I dreamt I was sleeping the last sleep, by that
       sleeper, with my heart stopped, and my cheek frozen against hers.' (p. 289)

Recalling his exhumation of Cathy's grave, Heathcliff's description of haunting (he
is almost possessed) encapsulates his relationship with Cathy, both before and after
her death. His dream of their reconciliation in the grave is at once touchingly
romantic and ghoulish. He has evidently found in the act of opening her grave a
release that will pave the way for his death and something approaching peace for his

long-tormented soul. He keeps alive the question of final rest, however, in the darkly humorous suggestion that he and Cathy may still not remain 'underground'.

(6)   'You know, I was wild after she died, and eternally, from dawn to dawn, praying her to return to me — her spirit — I have a strong faith in ghosts; I have a conviction that they can, and do exist, among us!' (p. 289)

Heathcliff is convinced of the existence of the supernatural. This is a powerful statement of faith, as his acknowledgement of this explains the continued experience he has had of Cathy since her death. Note the quasi-religious terms in which Heathcliff presents his views on the subject of ghosts.

(7)   ...the country folks, if you asked them, would swear on their Bible that he *walks*. There are those who speak to having met him near the church, and on the moor, and even within this house — Idle tales, you'll say, and so say I. Yet that old man by the kitchen fire affirms he has seen two on 'em, looking out of his chamber window, on every rainy night, since his death... (p. 336)

Nelly recounts to Lockwood the local belief that the ghosts of Heathcliff and Cathy walk together. We are far from convinced (as presumably is Lockwood, having himself experienced Cathy's visitation during his stay at the Heights) that these are idle tales.

Landscape and buildings

In the vast majority of novels, landscape and buildings are important to understanding the author's intentions. Within the Gothic novel, they take on an integral and symbolic significance. Consider the names of a selection of Gothic novels, and the impact of place is immediately apparent — *The Castle of Otranto*, *The Romance of the Forest*, *Northanger Abbey* and *The Mysteries of Udolpho* are a few examples. The other main method of naming a Gothic novel is after the central character, as in the case of *Vathek*, *Frankenstein*, *Melmoth the Wanderer*, *Uncle Silas* or *The Woman in Black*. *Wuthering Heights*, of course, falls within the former category, but the two naming methods together imply that place and character carry equal significance in Gothic works; indeed, many of the buildings and locations of these texts operate almost as characters in their own right.

Landscape is very important in *Wuthering Heights*. The rugged Yorkshire setting, with its violent weather and harsh landscape, is a suitable reflection of the events of the novel. The isolation of the location represents the isolation of the characters, and provides a suitable backdrop for the violent events of the novel — it is as if the place is beyond the bounds of conventional society and not subject to ordinary social conventions and demands. Similarly, the Heights itself takes on a life and a significance of its own in the course of the novel.

Examples and analysis

The following passage is Lockwood's initial description of Wuthering Heights. Consider what it suggests about the building and its inhabitants, looking closely at the language the author uses and considering the overtones of the details and images Brontë employs.

(1)   Wuthering Heights is the name of Mr Heathcliff's dwelling, 'Wuthering' being a significant provincial adjective, descriptive of the atmospheric tumult to which its station is exposed in stormy weather. Pure, bracing ventilation they must have up there, at all times, indeed: one may guess the power of the north wind, blowing over the edge, by the excessive slant of a few, stunted firs at the end of the house; and by a range of gaunt thorns all stretching their limbs one way, as if craving alms of the sun. Happily, the architect had foresight to build it strong: the narrow windows are deeply set in the wall, and the corners defended with large jutting stones.

   Before passing the threshold, I paused to admire a quantity of grotesque carving lavished over the front, and especially about the principal door, above which, among a wilderness of crumbling griffins, and shameless little boys, I detected the date '1500,' and the name 'Hareton Earnshaw.' I would have made a few comments, and requested a short history of the place from the surly owner, but his attitude at the door seemed to demand my speedy entrance, or complete departure, and I had no desire to aggravate his impatience, previous to inspecting the penetralium.

   One step brought us into the family sitting-room, without any introductory lobby, or passage: they call it here 'the house' pre-eminently. It includes kitchen and parlor, generally, but I believe at Wuthering Heights the kitchen is forced to retreat altogether into another quarter, at least I distinguished a chatter of tongues, and a clatter of culinary utensils, deep within; and I observed no signs of roasting, boiling, or baking, about the huge fire-place; nor any glitter of copper saucepans and tin cullenders on the walls. One end, indeed, reflected splendidly both light and heat from ranks of immense pewter dishes, interspersed with silver jugs and tankards, towering row after row, in a vast oak dresser, to the very roof. The latter had never been underdrawn; its entire anatomy lay bare to an inquiring eye, except where a frame of wood, laden with oatcakes, and clusters of legs of beef, mutton and ham, concealed it. Above the chimney were sundry villainous old guns, and a couple of horse-pistols, and, by way of ornament, three gaudily painted canisters disposed along its ledge. The floor was of smooth, white stone: the chairs, high-backed, primitive structures, painted green: one or two heavy black ones lurking in the shade. In an arch, under the dresser, reposed a huge, liver-coloured bitch pointer surrounded by a swarm of squealing puppies, and other dogs haunted other recesses. (pp. 4–5)

This description is immediately striking. The grotesque detail of the carving throws the reader at once into an atmosphere of Gothic excess and the bizarre. Brontë establishes that this is an ancient house, tantalisingly providing the name of Earnshaw as an initial point of entrance into the dark halls of the house and of the family history it embodies. This detail is confusing for the reader, who has just learnt that the house is owned by Mr Heathcliff.

The physical location is also central to our first impressions of the place; it is set in a landscape characterised by punishing weather, the significance of which soon becomes apparent when the reader is thrown into the violent domestic world of the novel.

The house is unlike other houses in the area; it is set apart by both its physical location and its nature. We are impressed by its grandeur, illustrated in the use of words such as 'lavished', which suggest richness and excess, but we cannot escape the dark and forbidding overtones of the word 'penetralium', which suggests the impenetrable depths of the house and, by extension, its inhabitants. The enormity of the house is suggested by the nameless voice coming from 'deep within'; its vastness adds to a lack of comfortable domesticity, illustrated in the absence of homely cooking utensils and the overpowering towers of tankards. Brontë person-ifies the building through her description of the deep, narrow windows, which are like squinting, deep-set eyes, always watching and evaluating, and overseeing the lives of the inhabitants.

Above all the reader cannot escape the uneasy sensation of pregnant threat suggested in phrases such as 'lurking in the shade', and the brooding presence of the unnumbered dogs. Such impressions are extended through her use of heavy and excessive colour — gaudy, green, black — and the violence suggested by the weapons.

(2)   There was a carpet, a good one; but the pattern was obliterated by dust; a fire-place
        hung with cut paper dropping to pieces; a handsome oak-bedstead with ample crimson
        curtains of rather expensive material, and modern make. But they had evidently experienced
        rough usage: the valances hung in festoons, wrenched from their rings, and the iron rod
        supporting them was bent in an arc, on one side, causing the drapery to trail upon the floor.
        The chairs were also damaged, many of them severely; and deep indentations deformed the
        panels of the walls. (p. 142)

In this description of Heathcliff's room, Brontë captures something of the mysterious complexity of the room's inhabitant. Its decayed wealth can be seen to symbolise the degradation both of the house and of Heathcliff himself; both were once noble or potentially noble, but have now fallen into a state of shabby (and tragic) disrepair. The dust in the room represents death and decay; this image comes to illustrate a deep truth about Heathcliff as the novel progresses, and the reader comes to realise the extent of his relationship with death and the decaying body of his beloved Cathy.

The presence of crimson in the room is another telling detail, clearly suggesting the presence of blood and violence, which play such a significant role in the novel, the tattered red curtains also demonstrate the crumbling wealth of the house. The imagery can be compared to that used at the start of *Jane Eyre*, when Jane is trapped in the Red Room. The damage to the room is a further indication of violent ill-usage and abuse, reflecting both the maltreatment Heathcliff received as a child, which has turned him into the bitter and twisted individual he is, and the destruction he has wreaked on the house, the world and the people with whom he comes into contact.

(3) 'And far rather would I be condemned to a perpetual dwelling in the infernal regions, than even for one night abide beneath the roof of Wuthering Heights again.' (p. 183)

Isabella is referring to Wuthering Heights. Note her suggestion that the building is worse than hell itself.

(4) He surveyed the carved front, and low-browed lattices; the straggling gooseberry bushes, and crooked firs, with solemn intentness, and then shook his head: his private feelings entirely disapproved of the exterior of his new abode... (p. 206)

Here the reader witnesses Linton's arrival at his father's house, Wuthering Heights. Note the personification of the building; 'low-browed' recalls the idea of narrow slit windows and therefore eyes, an image which is to gain increasing significance as the novel progresses, as Linton begins courting Catherine under the watchful gaze of Heathcliff. Notice too the clear implications of disorder in the use of words such as 'straggling' and 'crooked'.

(5) Catherine's face was just like the landscape — shadows and sunshine flitting over it, in rapid succession... (p. 266)

This sentence makes explicit the link between landscape and psychological state in the novel.

(6) ...the heat did not hinder me from enjoying the delightful scenery above and below; had I seen it nearer August, I'm sure it would have tempted me to waste a month among its solitudes. In winter, nothing more dreary, in summer, nothing more divine, than those glens shut in by hills, and those bluff, bold swells of heath. (pp. 305–06)

Upon his return to the wilds of Yorkshire, Lockwood reflects on the landscape in terms that encapsulate its contradictions. Brontë uses this as a symbol of the divided nature of the place and the people who live there.

(7) My walk home was lengthened by a diversion in the direction of the kirk. When beneath its walls, I perceived decay had made progress, even in seven months — many a window showed black gaps deprived of glass; and slates jutted off, here and there, beyond the right line of the roof, to be gradually worked off in coming autumn storms.

I sought, and soon discovered, the three head-stones on the slope next the moor — the middle one, grey, and half buried in heath — Edgar Linton's only harmonized by the turf, and moss creeping up its foot — Heathcliff's still bare.

I lingered round them, under that benign sky; watched the moths fluttering among the heath, and hare-bells; listened to the soft wind breathing through the grass; and wondered how anyone could ever imagine unquiet slumbers, for the sleepers in that quiet earth. (p. 337)

Here the reader is struck by the indeterminacy of the churchyard and its location. Brontë emphasises its decay, seeing in this a direct connection between the place and the three characters. The natural world and the graves' physical locations provide a symbolic reflection upon the characters and their relationship — Edgar is socially acceptable and as such lies 'in' the sanctified and tended land of the graveyard; Cathy is more suspect, and as such lies half 'in' and half 'out'; the social and moral outcast, Heathcliff, lies totally 'out'.

Critical voices

Gothic literature is a form that has proved consistently difficult to define. It has manifested itself in many different places and at many different times. In order to gain a fuller understanding of the form, therefore, it is helpful to bear in mind a range of the critical contexts within which Gothic literature has been read. The aim of this section is, by targeting a number of critical points of view, to provide a basis for thought and discussion when approaching any text within the Gothic tradition.

The nature of Gothic

The archaic and pagan

> Gothic was the archaic, the pagan, that which was prior to, or resisted the establishment of, civilised values and a well-regulated society. (David Punter, 1996)

Here, Punter suggests the essential historical connotations of the form, and emphasises the importance of the past. Gothic texts typically deal with a historical time past, as is seen in *The Castle of Otranto* (Horace Walpole), *The Monk* (Matthew Lewis) and *The Mysteries of Udolpho* (Ann Radcliffe). Other texts, such as the modern Gothic tales *The Woman in Black* and *The Mist in the Mirror* by Susan Hill and *Gormenghast* by Mervyn Peake, are set in an indeterminate time-world. A third group of texts, such as *Wuthering Heights*, *Frankenstein*, and Peter Ackroyd's *Hawksmoor*, veer between a present narrative and events related from the past. Note Punter's emphasis upon the 'external' and subversive nature of the genre. Gothic, he suggests, lies at the very boundaries of the acceptable; hence it is linked with a historically remote time, or with the religiously suspect (witchcraft, the pagan, non-Protestant religion), the exotic and the foreign. Even where the action of the texts is firmly located in England, the setting and events of the tales indicate the extent to which they represent values and demands that lie outside the bounds of the conventional and the acceptable. *Wuthering Heights* is set on the bleak and remote Yorkshire moors, while Susan Hill's *The Woman in Black* utilises the barren strangeness of the Eel Marsh to create its unholy and threatening atmosphere.

The bizarre and unfamiliar

> Gothic was chaotic...ornate and convoluted...excess and exaggeration, the product of the wild and uncivilised. (ibid.)

An essential element in Gothic is the uncontrollable and the excessive, the bizarre and the unfamiliar. It is the continual presence of such elements in Gothic texts that creates the sense of the unpredictable and the disturbing, the atmosphere of threat and foreboding. The representation of violent and extreme action and emotion, often incompletely explained, and the use of wild locations, creates a disturbing lack of security. The fictional world of *Wuthering Heights* makes considerable use of this.

The Gothic borderlands

> Gothic works, it is often objected, are not fully achieved works: they are fragmentary, inconsistent, jagged.... If Gothic works 'do not come out right', this is because they deal in psychological areas which themselves do not come out right, they deal in those structures of the mind which are compounded with repression rather than with the purified material to which realism claims access.... And it is here that we come to the crux of the matter: Gothic writers work — consciously or unconsciously — on the fringe of the acceptable, for it is on this borderland that fear resides. In the best works, the two sides of the border are grafted onto each other. (ibid.)

In this extract, Punter identifies the importance of uncertainty and incompleteness to the world view of the Gothic. The form itself reflects its content and concerns; the Gothic does not deal with the neat and the orderly, and therefore the works themselves are frequently neither neat nor orderly. Confusion as to action and motive are significant in that they indicate the very uncertainty and complexity with which the texts are seeking to engage. Heathcliff, Cathy and many of the other characters in *Wuthering Heights* are perfect examples of this. At the very heart of the novel and its many dilemmas and cruelties lies the peculiar inability of the characters to understand their own motivations, needs, desires and actions. Relationships within the closed communities of the Heights and the Grange, as well as with the wider world, prove deeply confusing and illustrate the importance of uncertainty within the text. The growing complexity of character connections and the disturbing cycles of repetition (almost inevitability) that Brontë's narrative invokes is central to the novel. Characters are frequently paired and associated with each other in the reader's consciousness, the result of which is that the distinctions between them become deliberately and increasingly uncertain as the novel progresses.

Gothic and social upheaval

The rise of Gothic occurred largely during periods of political unrest and social uncertainty. The great initial period of Gothic coincides with the French Revolution (1789) and the anti-Catholic Gordon Riots (1780). Around the same period came the turmoil and separation of the American War of Independence. Throughout subsequent literary history, the appearance of Gothic has continued to reflect periods of instability, or the fear of instability. Mervyn Peake's *Gormenghast* trilogy, for example, was written in the shadow of the Second World War, and the tales of Sir Arthur Conan Doyle and H. G. Wells reflect the fear of the 'outsider' bred by the colonial system.

> One of the most chilling fears that informs these stories is the threat of ancestral repetition.
> (Laura Kranzler, from *Introduction to Elizabeth Gaskell's Gothic Tales*, Penguin, 2000)

Wuthering Heights deals extensively not only with the possibility but also with the reality of generational repetition. Patterns of violence, revenge and death are visited upon successive generations of both the Earnshaws and the Lintons, households that are drawn ineluctably and inevitably closer together as the events of the novel develop. The most extended and obvious example of this is found in the close mirroring of events between the lives and characteristics of Cathy and her daughter Catherine, where even the name highlights the generational continuity.

Techniques of Gothic

Opposites and oppositions

> [The] juxtaposition of the ghastly and the everyday suggests one of the defining characteristics of the gothic genre, that of the uncanny double, the shadowy world that is the complex underbelly of familiar experience. (ibid.)

Kranzler illustrates the importance of opposites and opposition in the Gothic. She suggests the essentially subversive nature of the form and its importance in providing an alternative perception of reality.

Blurring the edges

> The Gothic was and remained the dimension of the imperfectly perceived.
> (David Punter, 1996)

Many Gothic narratives, including *Wuthering Heights*, gain considerable effect from blurring the edges of the narrative. Transitions between narrators and the varying perspectives they offer on events, along with the uncertainties engendered by paralleling the characters, create in the reader a sense of uncertainty and unease. This is a studied and deliberate effect, reflecting accurately the profound doubt and confusion underlying the form itself.

The forbidden and its attractions

> It is in its concern with paranoia, with barbarism and with taboo that the vital effort of Gothic fiction resides: these are the aspects of the terrifying to which the Gothic constantly and hauntedly returns. (ibid.)

Punter highlights the essential role of the forbidden and its attraction within the Gothic. *Wuthering Heights*, like many other Gothic texts, deals with the forbidden and the dangers of pursuing the forbidden. This raises questions about the reader's morality and pleasure in reading and enjoying these texts.

Distortion and exaggeration

> The Gothic is a distorting lens, a magnifying lens; but the shapes which we see through it have nonetheless a reality which cannot be apprehended in any other way. (ibid.)

This emphasises the importance of distortion and exaggeration in the Gothic. The larger-than-life and the twisted have a vital role to play, Punter suggests, in assisting the reader to approach certain less pleasant realities of life.

Gothic and religion

> These excluded areas…often retain a strong peripheral or inverted relationship with orthodox religion [and] embrace the practices usually termed occult. In such systems there is much more direct relationship with the invisible realms. (Clive Bloom, *Gothic Horror: A Reader's Guide from Poe to King and Beyond*, Macmillan, 1998)

This sheds an interesting light on the role of conventional religion in Gothic, a form which depends for much of its impact on a rejection of the orthodox and the establishment. Gothic fiction is notable for the frequent appearance of the devil and the devilish. The arcane and the forbidden is a staple element of Gothic authors, such as Peter Ackroyd, Charlotte Dacre and Matthew 'Monk' Lewis. It also has a key role to play in *Wuthering Heights*; Brontë writes of a world where values are inverted, and where the presentation of religion is at best unorthodox. Cathy and Heathcliff envisage a bizarre alternative heaven that they will inhabit together after their deaths, and Joseph is a figure of consummate religious hypocrisy. The church and its requirements remain a marginal and bizarre force within the novel, as in Lockwood's dream of Jabes Branderham and the grotesque graveyard scenes Heathcliff recounts. Brontë makes direct and extensive use of the language of hell and the satanic.

Realism and symbolism in Gothic

> Gothic fiction thus finds itself operating between two structural poles. On the one hand, because it rejects the account which realism gives of the world, it seeks to express truth through the use of other modes and genres — poetic prose, the recapture of tragedy, expressionistic writing, the revival of legend, the formation of quasi-myths — in order to

demonstrate that the individual's involvement with the world is not merely linear but is composed of moments with resonances and depths which can only be captured through the disruptive power of extensive metaphor and symbolism. (David Punter, 1996)

Note the importance of symbolism as opposed to realism within the Gothic. Brontë creates a fragile balance between the realistic and the symbolic. The relationship between the two is essential — a preponderance of either element leads to an imbalance and a consequent reduction in the impact of the writing and its ability to instil fear and uncertainty.

Gothic and the supernatural

…the power of the older Gothic…is to use the supernatural as an image for real and carefully depicted social fears. (ibid.)

This viewpoint emphasises the social/sociological function of Gothic. It suggests that the fear of social change and the socially suspect lies behind the use of the supernatural in Gothic fiction. The nebulous and indefinable nature of ghosts and monsters and their predatory, threatening tendencies play on the social, religious and political fears of the reader. Both Cathy and Heathcliff represent substantial threats to accepted norms of behaviour and social propriety and are both integrally linked with the supernatural throughout the novel.

Terror and horror

Terror and Horror are so far opposite, that the first expands the soul and awakens the faculties to a higher degree of life; the other contracts, freezes and nearly annihilates them. I apprehend that neither Shakespeare nor Milton by their fictions, nor Mr Burke by his reasoning, anywhere looked to positive horror as a source of the sublime, though they all agree that terror is a very high one; and where lies the great difference between terror and horror, but in uncertainty and obscurity, that accompany the first, respecting the dreaded evil? (Ann Radcliffe, from 'On the Supernatural in Poetry', 1816)

The difference between terror and horror is a key distinction as far as Radcliffe is concerned. She uses it to point to the morally elevating and uplifting potential of terror, as opposed to the morally and spiritually enervating impact of horror. Devendra Varma was one of the first critics to seize on this distinction, characterising the difference between terror and horror as the difference between 'awful apprehension and sickening realisation'. Robert Hume has also embraced this distinction, although in slightly different terms; he argues that the horror novel replaces the ambiguous physical details of the terror novel with a more disturbing set of moral and psychological ambiguities. Robert L. Platzner, while not challenging entirely the difference between terror and horror, notes where the edges blur. He refers specifically to the writings of Ann Radcliffe, but the application is more general: 'It appears that far from never crossing the boundary between terror and horror, Mrs Radcliffe compulsively places her heroine in situations of overwhelming anxiety in which a gradual shift from terror to horror is inescapable.' This links directly to the situations of many of Brontë's characters in *Wuthering Heights*, who find themselves repeatedly subjected to cruelty, brutality and fear.

Freud, Marx and feminism

Three of the most significant critical movements of the last century have been based on the writings and theories of Sigmund Freud, Karl Marx and the feminist movement. All three approaches cast an interesting light on a reading of *Wuthering Heights*, a novel that provides rich potential for a wide range of interpretations.

Sigmund Freud

Sigmund Freud (1856–1939), a psychoanalyst, formulated his theories in a series of books, *The Interpretation of Dreams* being the most well-known. His work led to many interesting developments in the literary world, including the rise of the psychoanalytic school of literary criticism, which has been highly influential. He is most famous for propounding the concepts of the Oedipus complex (an innate sexual attraction to the parent of the opposite gender), the death wish, a focus upon the phallus as a symbol and its corollary, penis envy, as well as the formulation of the divisions within the human psyche. His ideas and their appearance within Freudian literary criticism relate in detail to the fictional world of *Wuthering Heights*.

Childhood

Freud's concentration on infancy as the basis for subsequent psychological development is highly significant. Throughout the novel, Nelly Dean focuses on the progress of the children of the Earnshaw and Linton households. Considerable importance is attached to the varied home environments within which the children of the households grow up. Cathy is changed forever by her stay at the Grange with the Lintons, and the differences between Heathcliff and Edgar are invoked repeatedly. Heathcliff's uncertain parentage and early childhood, and his hard upbringing in the Earnshaw household where he suffers at the hands of the natural children, twists his character and marks him forever. In his turn, he deliberately terrorises his own son, Linton, and brutalises Hareton, who falls into his care after the death of Hindley Earnshaw. Standing *in loco parentis*, he calculatedly fails in his parental duties of nurture and affection, leading to a continuation of the cycle of revenge within the novel.

Sexuality

Freud believed that sexuality, repressed or otherwise, lies at the root of human behaviour. In *Wuthering Heights* considerable emphasis is placed on sex and sexuality. The most powerful examples of this are seen in the relationship of Heathcliff and Cathy, and its contrast with the relationship between Cathy and Edgar. The passion between Heathcliff and Cathy is one of the most striking elements of the novel for many readers. The animal-like ferocity of their physical contact, teetering always on the brink of the desire to inflict physical pain, brings violence into romance in a daring and highly provocative way. Nelly Dean is unable to account for such manifestations of passion as they are alien to her experience. Cathy certainly sees her personality and her very being as totally embodied in Heathcliff: as she famously observes, 'I *am* Heathcliff!' Interestingly, the relationship remains unconsummated until the bizarre union in the grave. By contrast, the relationship between Cathy and Edgar is an apparently passionless affair, lacking the fire of her contact with Heathcliff, although it is, nevertheless, consummated, leading to the birth of Catherine. There is a certain significance in that Cathy dies so shortly after the birth of her daughter, as if further sexual contact between her and Edgar is inappropriate.

Emphasis on the Oedipal relationship between parents and children is at the heart of Freud's theory and also relates significantly to *Wuthering Heights*. Linton Heathcliff, for example, seeks to re-establish, under his father's guidance, the relationship that existed between Heathcliff and Isabella. The convergence of the houses of Earnshaw and Linton also points towards a close-knit, almost incestuous web of relationships with all of its implicit Oedipal connotations.

The self

The psychology of the divided self is a further crucial element in Freud's theory. He identifies a three-way division of the human psyche into the 'id' (appetite-driven desires), the 'ego' (conscious sense of 'self' and awareness of others) and the 'super-ego' (sense of morality, sometimes seen as conscience). In *Wuthering Heights*, Brontë pursues her characters through their stages of development, and Freud's divisions illuminate their growth into adulthood, and the role of the warring elements of the self. Brontë also presents the divided and deeply flawed nature of Heathcliff and many of the other characters through the device of character doubling; this enables the reader to almost perceive an externalisation of the conflicting elements of the human mind. The most overt example of this is the 'division' (or multiplication) of Cathy into Cathy Linton/Earnshaw/Heathcliff.

The death wish

Freud saw the death wish as a powerful psychological drive, based on a continuing desire to return to the womb. This can be linked to Gothic's frequent use of dark, enclosed spaces, e.g. coffins. The garret where Lockwood sleeps and the enclosed wooden bed, for example, is like a nightmarish womb. After the birth of Catherine, Cathy achieves death, wishing vindictively that her death may inflict suffering and haunting on Heathcliff. Indeed, Heathcliff is subsequently locked in a pursuit to the death of an image of his lost love and his hoped-for reunion with her. On a number of occasions he expresses the wish that his sufferings in being separated from Cathy could be ended by death. Death is apparently never far away in the brutal world of the novel.

Karl Marx

Karl Marx (1818–83) is best known for his great work *Das Kapital*, in which, with Friedrich Engels, he launched an outspoken attack on the capitalist system. His concept of 'historical materialism' has been highly influential in the Marxist school of literary criticism; this school seeks to understand literature as a form of material production that participates in and illuminates the processes of history.

There are many perceived social or political 'messages' within *Wuthering Heights*. The novel clearly poses questions regarding the implications of social inclusion/exclusion and its consequences. The text highlights particularly the dangers of social isolation and the consequences of domestic tyranny. Brontë also looks at the issue of female inheritance rights and the threats posed to women within a dominant male hierarchy.

The particular historical and sociological period in which Brontë wrote the novel can be linked to the key Marxist concept of class struggle. *Wuthering Heights* was written in a time of political uncertainty between the two electoral Reform Acts. This was a period of social and class upheaval in England, and a time when the rights of women were beginning to be considered.

Readers of *Wuthering Heights* need to consider how the plot, characters and settings reflect the concept of class struggle, either by inclusion or omission. The novel is keenly aware of issues of class; Brontë makes very clear the threat posed to the status quo by the socially suspect Heathcliff. As an adoptive son of the Earnshaws, he enjoys the status and rights of the gentry, but remains distinctly separate from them — a fact of which they continually remind him. He is a thorn in the flesh of the established landowners. The novel also considers the rights of inheritance in the female line; Edgar seeks to protect Catherine and her inheritance from the predatory intentions of Heathcliff who, after the death of his son Linton, becomes the next in the male line to inherit the Grange.

A final key concept here is the way that, through class struggle, characters become 'outsider' figures and alienated from society. Many characters in *Wuthering Heights* are interlopers: Lockwood is isolated socially; Heathcliff fights for, but never establishes, his right to be accepted within the society he inhabits; the Heights and the Grange remain isolated and have very little contact with the social world of Gimmerton and beyond.

Feminism

Feminism is a modern tradition of literary criticism and polemic devoted to the defence of women's writing or of female fictional characters against the condescension of a predominantly male literary establishment. Significantly, Emily Brontë and her sisters, Charlotte and Anne, provide in their novels some of the most profound and most sustained proposals and defences of the female cause. A number of ideas central to the feminist point of view are highly relevant to *Wuthering Heights*.

The relative silence and passivity of female characters in Gothic texts have been noted by many critics. *Wuthering Heights* challenges many of the typical perceptions of women in Gothic; this is a violent domestic world where women give as good as they get. Cathy, Catherine, Isabella and Nelly Dean are all strong women who refuse to remain silent in the face of their maltreatment, and Mrs Earnshaw, although present in the text only briefly, gives every impression of being a dominant figure in her household. The women in the novel are no more helpless when confronted with the power of Heathcliff than are many of the male characters.

The stereotyping of female characters according to male fantasy is another criticism levelled at a wide range of texts. In *Wuthering Heights*, while Cathy, Catherine and Isabella are all beauties, they do not conform to traditional models of propriety, and certainly do not take on the extreme and extended passivity characteristic of so many Gothic females.

The concerns and plights of women are dealt with in a number of Gothic texts. *Wuthering Heights* deals extensively with the issue of domestic violence, which is frequently (though not exclusively) directed at women. It highlights too the problem of inequality within inheritance law, and the difficulties and dangers this often put women under. Even though many of the women in the novel are strong characters, they are still largely obliged to live under the 'protection' of males.

Quotations

Consider each of the following quotations, all of which could be used to give key evidence in essay answers. Identify which character is speaking in each and its context. Then consider which arguments or points of view you might use each quotation to support in the course of an essay response.

(p. 4)	Wuthering Heights is the name of Mr Heathcliff's dwelling, 'Wuthering' being a significant provincial adjective, descriptive of the atmospheric tumult to which its station is exposed in stormy weather.
(p. 46)	We don't in general take to foreigners here, Mr Lockwood, unless they take to us first.
(p. 66)	...he cursed and defied — he execrated God and man, and gave himself up to reckless dissipation.
(p. 66)	I could not half tell what an infernal house we had.
(p. 102)	'Tell her what Heathcliff is — an unreclaimed creature, without refinement — without cultivation; an arid wilderness of furze and whinstone.'
(p. 136)	'Is Mr Heathcliff a man? If so, is he mad? And if not, is he a devil?'
(p. 144)	'...I assure you, a tiger, or a venomous serpent could not rouse terror in me equal to that which he wakens.'
(p. 183)	'...far rather would I be condemned to a perpetual dwelling in the infernal regions, than even for one night abide beneath the roof of Wuthering Heights again.'
(p. 222)	'...Mr Heathcliff dislikes me; and is a most diabolical man, delighting to wrong and ruin those he hates, if they give him the slightest opportunity.'
(p. 253)	'...I feel so cross and bitter, I hate everybody!'
(p. 254)	'He'll never let his friends be at ease, and he'll never be at ease himself!'
(p. 266)	Catherine's face was just like the landscape — shadows and sunshine flitting over it, in rapid succession...
(p. 288)	'Mr Heathcliff, *you* have *nobody* to love you; and, however miserable you make us, we shall still have the revenge of thinking that your cruelty rises from your greater misery!'
(p. 288)	...she seemed to have made up her mind to enter into the spirit of her future family, and draw pleasure from the griefs of her enemies.
(p. 333)	'...I'm too happy, and yet I'm not happy enough. My Soul's bliss kills my body, but does not satisfy itself.'
(p. 335)	...I tried to close his eyes — to extinguish, if possible, that frightful, life-like gaze of exultation, before anyone else beheld it. They would not shut — they seemed to sneer at my attempts, and his parted lips, and sharp, white teeth sneered too!

Literary terms

The terms and concepts below have been selected for their relevance to writing about *Wuthering Heights*. It will aid argument and expression to become familiar with them and to use them in your essays.

allegory	extended metaphor conveying moral meaning
allusion	reference, either direct or indirect, to other texts
antithesis	contrast of ideas expressed by parallelism
black humour	makes fun of something serious
caricature	grotesque exaggeration in portrayal of character
characterisation	the ways in which an author creates and develops a character
contextuality	historical, cultural, social, economic and political background of a text
didactic	adjective applied to a work of literature setting out to promote or teach a particular religious, political or philosophical point of view
epigraph	inscription at the head of a chapter or book
episodic	narrative is divided into individual events
epistolary	taking the form of letters
first-person narrative	story told from the 'I' point of view
genre	type or form of writing
imagery	descriptive or figurative language; often appeals to a variety of the senses — touch, taste, smell, sight, sound
irony	language intended to mean the opposite of the words actually employed; an amusing or cruel reversal of a situation
juxtaposition	placing ideas, characters or events side by side for (often ironic) contrast or to create other types of literary connection
myth	fiction about supernatural beings
narrative structure	way in which a story is organised; may be chronological, reverse chronological, episodic, flashbacks etc.
omniscient narrator	a narrator who has God-like powers to see all events, actions, motivations and thoughts
parable	story used to illuminate a moral lesson
pathetic fallacy	use of the weather or the landscape to reflect events, moods etc.
pathos	sad situation, evoking pity in the reader
personification	attribution of human qualities to objects, ideas etc.
plurality	possibility of multiple meanings of text
register	level of formality in expression
stereotype	typical characteristics of a category of person, often used for mockery
symbolism	use of characters, actions, objects to represent abstract concepts

synopsis	plot summary
third person narrative	story told from the 'he/she/it' point of view
tragedy	literary work that traces the downfall of a protagonist — often this character is initially seen as 'better' than the rest of us
unreliable narrator	a narrator the reader does not feel able to trust (due to age, naïvety, self-delusion, tendency to lie, political reasons etc.)

Questions & Answers

Essay planning and examiner comments

This section looks closely at a number of examination essay titles. Possible plans are given to outline how the titles may be approached. These are suggested responses only and other points or approaches may be equally valid. They also represent much longer plans than would be realistic for an examination essay, aiming to give a fuller coverage of relevant material. In addition, of course, the points identified would need to be illustrated carefully with well-chosen examples and quotation from the text. Accompanying each plan is a selective breakdown of the mark schemes specific to the tasks to demonstrate requirements for grades A and C. These extracts illustrate clearly how the Assessment Objectives (see pages 2–3) are applied by examiners.

1 **Look again at Volume I, Chapter I of the novel. Then answer the following questions.**
   - **What do you learn about the character of Lockwood in this chapter?**
   - **How does Emily Brontë's method of telling the story engage your interest in this chapter?**
   - **Some readers find Lockwood an uninspiring narrator who tells a good tale in spite of himself. What do you think Brontë achieves through using Lockwood as a narrator here and elsewhere in the text?**

Possible plan

Lockwood's character

Lockwood is a romantic idealist. He has a keen sense of naïvety, or possibly irony — note his initial comments on Heathcliff as 'A capital fellow!'. He is gentlemanly and polite — this sets him radically apart from Heathcliff and the other characters, and as such he is an isolated outsider. He is interested in all he sees around him — the landscape and people, and is observant — he gives a detailed description of the Heights. He feels confused — a confusion the reader will come to share with him — about the history and complex relationships of the Grange and the Heights. He gives a (surprisingly) perceptive response to Heathcliff as a man who will 'love and hate, equally under cover'. He is bewildered by the dogs' attack and the brutal amusement of the inhabitants. Overall, he is naïve, complacent, educated, curious, and generally a poor judge of character.

Brontë's storytelling

Brontë draws on contrasts — the difference between appearance and reality in Heathcliff is established immediately. Note the juxtaposition of Lockwood's gentility and the brutality of the Heights. She creates an air of brooding menace; the dogs, like the inhabitants, suggest imminent threat. Her description of the Heights is intriguing — it is a place brooding darkness, and connections are drawn with Heathcliff's character. An atmosphere of violence is established. Uncertainty is created about the history of the house, through the inscription over the door. Grotesquerie and elements of the Gothic develop a sense of foreboding. The differences between Heathcliff and Lockwood are intriguing to the reader. Brontë employs a vocabulary of darkness and brutality; Lockwood's gentlemanly terms and the consciously literary language of description contrast with Joseph's dialect.

Readers' responses

Lockwood is one of a number of narrators. His is a frame narrative within which Nelly Dean and others weave the tale. As an outsider to the novel's events, he is near to the position of the reader, and Brontë uses this to create a sense of strangeness and discomfort in the tale's dark and troubled world. She also uses him as a way into the confusion of names and history of the Earnshaws and the Lintons. He is at once engaged in the shockingly brutal world of the novel, which makes him eager to hear Nelly's explanation. Lockwood tends to fade in the face of the events he recounts, but he is humorous and likeable. He tells a tale of personal growth, which applies to himself and to the rest of the characters in the novel.

Mark scheme

Grade C

AO2i   ability to reflect on meanings, sustaining and developing ideas; clear understanding of character, illustrated by textual reference

AO3   understanding of how language contributes to meaning (e.g. contrast of educated, literary language and dialect); use of description

AO4   awareness of other possible interpretations; offers opinion on Lockwood

AO5i   clearly explains Lockwood's role in the novel; clear references to other parts of the novel and other narrators

Grade A

AO2i   confident selection of material and excellent understanding of character of Lockwood

AO3   conceptualised discussion of presentational devices and their effect on the reader

AO4   cogent argument about the role of Lockwood's narrative; develops links with other narratives and the effect of this; considers themes (e.g. reconciliation, rebirth and growth)

AO5i   conceptualised link between this chapter and the novel as a whole

2 Look again at Volume II, Chapter I. Then answer the following questions:
  - What emotions are experienced by Heathcliff and Catherine in this chapter?
  - Comment on the way this chapter is written.
  - Some readers see the romantic elements of the novel as the most memorable. How important do you think such elements are?

Possible plan

Emotions

The chapter is full of violent shifts and contrasting emotions. Catherine is a mass of mixed emotions and 'constantly varying caprices'. She is almost 'unearthly' and lethargic at one moment, full of passionate energy and 'wild vindictiveness' the next. Her physical state is testament to the destructive nature of her passions. Heathcliff is full of impatience, grief, despair, forgiveness, resentment and surprising restraint by turns. Brontë achieves a powerful impact on the reader by juxtaposing and continually shifting the emotional responses of the characters. Other emotions include: sentimentality; powerful and wordless love; agony; anger and harsh words; unbearable pain; burning intensity; lack of pity; the desire to inflict mutual suffering. As Nelly observes, Brontë draws a 'strange and fearful picture'.

How the chapter is written

The detachment and emotional coolness of Lockwood's brief introduction contrasts almost comically with the fiery passion of the scene that follows. The scene is filtered through the perception of Nelly Dean — it is very voyeuristic. Contrast and juxta-position are to the fore as presentational devices. This scene begins at a window — it is one of many significant 'window' scenes in the novel (compare the ghostly appearance of Cathy at the beginning of the novel and Heathcliff's return from Cathy's grave) which bear great symbolic weight. Brontë uses both the verbal and the physical to great effect, often to the extent of causing physical pain (e.g. embraces, grinding teeth, seizing and tearing hair, inflicting bruises). There is extensive use of extremes and excess. The imagery of animal-like behaviour, imprisonment, life and death, heaven and hell is used throughout — note the deployment of contrast again here.

Importance of romantic aspects

Romantic elements in the novel are certainly both central and of considerable impact. The bizarre romance of Cathy and Heathcliff is shocking, brutal, tragic, passionate and undeniably powerful. Their love is far from conventional. Heathcliff is an unusual and deeply troubling version of the Byronic hero, as Cathy is an equally unconventional heroine of romance. Both draw significant elements of their nature and their relationship from the Gothic and its tradition of attractive villains. The covert sexuality of their meetings is similar to scenes from *Dracula*. Love and the desire to inflict pain, to relate and to revenge are inextricably linked in a mutually destructive passion. The dichotomy of attraction and repulsion is at the heart of their relationship and the novel as a whole. Other readers may see the brutality and violence of the text as the most salient feature. Historical and social contextual features are important too.

Mark scheme

Grade C

AO2i   clear and well-illustrated understanding of emotions demonstrated in the chapter; identifies clearly a range of these (e.g. rage, pain, love, hatred, grief, fear)

AO3   clear discussion of presentational features (Nelly's perspective, contrast, window imagery, emotive language, imagery and vocabulary of imprisonment, heaven/hell etc.)

AO4   beginnings of awareness of others' informed opinions and interpretations; states a view on importance of romantic elements in the novel

AO5i   clearly explains importance of romance in context of whole text; may begin to identify other central characteristics of the text

Grade A

AO2i   secure; confidently ranges around text; excellent understanding and exploration of emotions displayed; excellent supporting reference

AO3   excellent exploration of the role of language and its contribution to effect and meaning in the chapter

AO4   cogently constructed argument about significance of romantic elements, engaging with and/or challenging view that they are most memorable

AO5i   conceptualised response to context and detailed awareness of other contexts for reading and interpretation

Examination essay titles

The titles that follow can be used for planning practice, full essay-writing practice or both. They may be used as a basis for class discussion and collaborative work, or on an individual basis for timed or extended writing. You should be aware of the need in all responses to refer closely to the text, supporting your arguments and comments with succinct and relevant evidence. Where appropriate, you may also choose to incorporate relevant critical material as a basis for your argument and response.

Whole-text-based essay questions

1 How far and why do you consider *Wuthering Heights* to be a moral tale and how far an immoral one?

2 "'My love for Heathcliff resembles the eternal rocks beneath...I *am* Heathcliff — he's always, always in my mind — not as a pleasure, any more than I am always a pleasure to myself — but, as my own being'" (p. 82). How far do you find Cathy's comments a satisfactory definition of her relationship with Heathcliff?

3 '*Wuthering Heights* was hewn in a wild workshop, with simple tools, out of homely materials. The statuary found a granite block on a solitary moor...With time and labour, the crag took human shape; and there it stands colossal' (Charlotte Brontë). What do you find particularly interesting in this view, and how do you relate it to the novel and its impact upon the reader?

4 'Gothic was chaotic...ornate and convoluted...excess and exaggeration, the product of the wild and uncivilised' (David Punter). How far do you consider *Wuthering Heights* to be a text written within the Gothic tradition, and how far do you find Punter's comments helpful in understanding the novel?

5 How far and in what ways does Brontë succeed in making the reader feel sorry for Heathcliff?

Prescribed passage-based questions

Examiners advise that a substantial portion (up to 60%) of responses to passage-based questions should refer to the rest of the work being studied. Focus on the passage selected, but refer to events which precede and follow it, too. It is essential to demonstrate how the passage operates within the wider novel. Establish the context of the passage and why it is a significant moment in the text. Then go on to explore how it links to the rest of the novel in terms of character, plot, theme, technique and so on. Where a specified aspect of the passage, such as an author's use of language or imagery, is identified, ensure that this is a central element in your response.

1 Read the section: 'He entered, vociferating oaths dreadful to hear...with my precious charge pressed to my heart' (pp. 74–75). Comment in detail on Brontë's choice of language and use of violence, and how this links to the domestic scene she presents, both in this passage and in the novel as a whole.

2 Remind yourself of the passage: "'Is Mr Heathcliff a man?...and shut and re-fastened the door'" (pp. 136–38). Identify how this passage seems to capture and present the main concerns of the novel, paying particular attention to devices that may be considered typical of the Gothic tradition.

3 Look closely at the section: 'Nobody but I even did him the kindness to call him a dirty boy... "'I shall be as dirty as I please, and I like to be dirty, and I will be dirty'"' (p. 55). Explore the ways in which Brontë presents the relationship between Cathy and Heathcliff here. How does this relate to the rest of the novel?

4 Read the following passage: "'I got a spade from the toolhouse, and began to delve with all my might...till that old rascal Joseph, no doubt, believed that my conscience was playing the fiend inside of me'" (pp. 289–91). What impression does Brontë give her reader here of Heathcliff's character, and how does this relate to the view created of him in the novel as a whole?

5 Refresh your memory of the following section: 'I listened doubtingly an instant...a light glimmered through the squares at the top of the bed' (pp. 24–26). Discuss the relationship between the real world and the dream world in this passage. How do you find this significant to the novel as whole?

Selected passage-based essays

When a task gives the option of selecting your own passages for specific reference, it is essential to select carefully. Failure to do so can lead to digression and even irrelevance. Ensure that the passages you choose are identified clearly for the reader and that they enable you to address the issues raised in the question specifically and in detail. Remember, the passages you remember and/or like best are not necessarily the most appropriate choices.

1 Select and comment on two or three passages which illustrate Emily Brontë's use of nature and natural description in *Wuthering Heights*. Consider the beauty and harshness of the natural world, and the symbolic significance of nature in the meaning and effect of the novel as a whole.

2 Choose two or three episodes which focus on Heathcliff. Demonstrate the ways in which Brontë uses these episodes to display the contrasting elements within his character.

3 Select two or three passages where Brontë makes use of violence and brutality. Explore how she presents this violence to the reader, how she creates her effects and the impact the use of violence has on the novel as a whole.

4 Choose two or three passages where the doubling of characters appears to you to be particularly significant. Explain the effect of each of these examples on the reader and explore the reasons for Brontë's use of the device within *Wuthering Heights*.

5 Select two or three passages where the supernatural intrudes into the novel. Explain the role of the supernatural in *Wuthering Heights*, considering its impact upon the characters and upon the reader, and the role of elements of the Gothic in the text.

Sample essays

Below are two sample essays of different types by different students. They have both been assessed as falling within the band for grade A. You can judge them against the Assessment Objectives for your exam board and decide on the mark you think each deserves and why. The examiner comments after each essay point out ways in which each could be improved in terms of content, style and accuracy.

Sample essay 1

Select and comment on two passages that illustrate Emily Brontë's presentation of extreme passion in *Wuthering Heights*. In your answer you should:
- **explore and explain your own views of the feelings in the passages you have chosen**
- **look closely at the use of language, setting and action to develop emotion**
- **discuss questions about the genre of *Wuthering Heights***

Extreme passion is a fundamental component of *Wuthering Heights*. Often the passion portrayed is so profound that the characters cannot themselves understand the depth or nature of the emotions they are experiencing, nor can they control the ways in which such passion manifests itself. Throughout the novel Brontë creates situations of considerable tension as individuals fight to define, defend and comprehend themselves in the claustrophobic atmosphere of the Grange and the Heights. The harshness of life on the barren moors and the grinding isolation faced by all the characters of the novel are both the cause and the effect of the violent emotions felt by the characters. The frequent use Brontë makes of such passion demonstrates the influences of both sentimental and Gothic fiction in *Wuthering Heights*, forms which make regular use of extreme and shifting emotion.

One of the most striking examples of excessive passion in the novel is the final meeting between Heathcliff and Cathy before Cathy's death in the opening chapter of Volume II. Even before Heathcliff enters the room, Brontë alerts the reader to the powerful emotional charge that hangs in the air. Cathy, we are told, listens 'breathlessly' and with 'straining eagerness' for Heathcliff's arrival, whose approach is announced by purposeful footsteps and the trying of door handles. The delayed identification of the visitor serves to heighten still further the reader's and Cathy's emotional tension. When Heathcliff eventually enters the bedchamber, the full tide of excess emotion breaks; unexpectedly, however, it breaks not in noise and words but in silence. The wordless passion with which the meeting takes place is an extremely powerful intimation of the unity between Cathy and Heathcliff. No words are needed to express their feelings for one another, but equally no words could express such a passion. The extent of their emotion is emphasised by the length of their embrace, which lasts 'for some five minutes', and by the countless kisses that Heathcliff bestows on Cathy. The impact of their meeting is revealed when Brontë adds that Heathcliff 'could hardly bear, for downright agony, to look into her face' and his eyes 'burned with anguish'.

This is not a conventional love scene. The fierceness of the passion displayed by Cathy and Heathcliff creates discomfort in both the reader and the watching Nelly. In contrast to her formerly feeble state, Cathy becomes reanimated as she approaches death in Heathcliff's presence. This demonstrates the power of the passion that exists between them — it is a passion that defies both life and death, as Heathcliff's haunted misery after Cathy's death makes clear. They are almost literally a source of life for each other. Heathcliff refers to Cathy as 'my life', a phrase that echoes Cathy's prior claim that 'I *am* Heathcliff'. So intense is their mutual passion that their only means of self-definition is through each other. As the scene progresses, violence of passion transmogrifies into actual violence.

Integral to their relationship is the need to inflict pain — both psychological and physical — on each other. This emerges early in the narrative, and is no less evident at this definitive point in their relationship. Cathy's emotional response to Heathcliff's presence is so violent that she 'seized' his hair and 'retained…a portion of the locks she had been grasping'. Heathcliff, too, displays physical harshness, in spite of Cathy's fatal condition. Nelly records how he grabs Cathy by the arm 'and so inadequate was his stock of gentleness to the requirements of her condition, that on his letting go, I saw four distinct impressions left blue in the colourless skin'. Such physical brutality is a direct reflection of the emotional violence the characters suffer.

Throughout the passage Brontë employs vocabulary that emphasises this. Words such as 'vindictiveness', 'savagely', 'wrenching' and 'grinding' all serve to reinforce the reader's sense of the extreme passions at play here. The meeting in Cathy's bedchamber, a place full of sexual charge, is more like the meeting of two beasts than of two lovers. Nelly is awestruck by the 'strange and fearful picture' they make, and observes how at one point Heathcliff 'gnashed at me, and foamed like a mad dog, and gathered her to him with greedy jealousy'. The pair can never truly meet; rather they must collide. It is because of this, perhaps, that the infliction of pain becomes a necessary part of their relationship. This is illustrated when Cathy cries, in the heat of her tormented passion, 'I care nothing for your sufferings!' Set against the mores of early Victorian society and its conventional romantic demands and lovers' codes, such a scene must have appeared shocking indeed.

The following chapter provides an excellent example of Brontë's use of extremes of passion, too. Throughout the novel Heathcliff is an ambiguous figure — at times evoking dislike, at others commanding deep sympathy — and Brontë employs this dichotomy to great effect in this episode. In the wake of Cathy's death, he is profoundly distressed and we are forced to feel sorry for him, in spite of all his brutality. Nelly reflects that he is a 'poor wretch' who has 'a heart and nerves the same as your brother men!' Natural emotional responses, however, are not enough to contain Heathcliff's feelings and it soon becomes evident that his reaction to Cathy's death is far from that to be expected from other men.

The news that Cathy died peacefully and Nelly's pious wish that she may wake in the peace of heaven meets with a violent and shocking response of 'frightful vehemence' and is followed by 'a paroxysm of ungovernable passion'. Even from beyond the grave, Cathy continues to exert her strange influence over Heathcliff, a situation he actively seeks in begging her spirit to 'haunt me, then…. Be with me always — take any form — drive me mad! Only *do* not leave me in this abyss where I cannot find you!' They remain inseparable, even though death has come between them, as Heathcliff reiterates: 'I *cannot* live without my life! I *cannot* live without my soul!' This emphasises the all-consuming nature of their love and his all-consuming grief at the loss of Cathy.

As is so often the case in this novel, the psychological finds its manifestation in the physical. In this scene, Heathcliff's emotional pain has to be matched by physical pain. This is first inflicted upon himself. After he leaves the Grange, Nelly watches as he 'dashed his head against the knotted trunk; and, lifting up his eyes, howled, not like a man, but like a savage beast getting goaded to death with knives and spears', and the trunk of the tree remains stained with his blood. Yet self-hurt cannot contain Heathcliff's emotions, as we see when Heathcliff nearly murders Hindley in the aftermath of Cathy's funeral.

Wuthering Heights is a novel of extraordinary passion. It moves far beyond the confines of the conventional Romantic novel, drawing on many of the devices of the Gothic novel, the dark underbelly of the Romantic era. Throughout the novel emotions are over-whelmingly present, heightened by the claustrophobia of the domestic environment of the Heights and the Grange. The characters cannot escape the cycle of emotion within the narrow social world they inhabit, and they must struggle to prevent the apparently inevitable repetition of horrific events from one generation to another. The pairing of Heathcliff and Cathy stands astride the whole novel as the embodiment of overpowering and frequently irrational emotion, which damages not only themselves but all who come into contact with them. It is only with Heathcliff's death that a new hope emerges and the possibility of emotional stability returns.

Sample essay 2

Discuss the concept of division in *Wuthering Heights*.

Wuthering Heights, Emily Brontë's only novel, bears many of the traits of the Gothic novel, a form that thrives on the existence of opposition and division. Such concerns lie at the very heart of the text and operate on a variety of levels. As her tale unfolds, Brontë explores their impact on the individual, on relationships, on the family unit and on society as a whole.

From the very outset, division is an important concept. Lockwood, who has recently arrived in the region as the new tenant at Thrushcross Grange, observes that the locale is: 'A perfect misanthropist's Heaven — and Mr Heathcliff and I are such a suitable pair to divide the desolation between us.' This significantly establishes the theme of division in the reader's mind. A seemingly innocent observation at first sight, it actually serves to illustrate a number of more disturbing possibilities. As the chapter progresses, Heathcliff's aggressive and solitary nature begins to emerge, demonstrating the extent to which he is set apart from local society and his new neighbour. A gentleman by birth, Lockwood contrasts strikingly with the coarser and harsher character of Heathcliff even at this early stage, before the reader is aware of his provenance. Furthermore, it suggests the presence of important and even threatening distinctions to be drawn between the worlds of the Heights and the Grange that the two men inhabit.

As the novel continues, the concept of social division continues to be important. The Lintons, the inhabitants of Thrushcross Grange, are evidently the social superiors of the Earnshaws, who live at Wuthering Heights, a wild and desolate house on the very top of the moors. Brontë uses the unreclaimed wildness of the location of the Heights to suggest the wildness of its inhabitants and the events that will occur there in the course of the novel. Heathcliff, the wildest of all the characters in the text, may be the owner of the Grange, but he can never live or be welcome there. This much is made clear early in the novel, when he and Cathy are caught one night spying through the windows of the Grange; Cathy is made to stay with the Lintons — an experience which significantly begins the process of her separation from Heathcliff — while her companion, a suspect 'gypsy brat', is driven from the place to return to the Heights alone. The strong identity of the family unit and the close-knit exclusivity of local society allows no place for outsiders such as Heathcliff; even 'acceptable' strangers like Lockwood are made to feel that they fall the wrong side of the divide. As Nelly Dean informs him: 'We don't in general take to foreigners here, Mr Lockwood, unless they take to us first.'

Brontë is not only concerned with social division, however. Familial division is also important throughout the novel. As we have seen already, there exists a significant division between the Linton and Earnshaw families, suggested in the very nature of the houses they inhabit. Division *within* families is also significant, however, as can be seen when Mr Earnshaw brings Heathcliff home from a journey to Liverpool. Heathcliff, a suspect outsider, whose race is never firmly established, sows the seeds of dissent within the Earnshaw household from the very night of his arrival. Similarly, Isabella's determination to marry Heathcliff later in the novel leads to a harmful and isolating split with her brother, Edgar.

Yet the novel does not only deal with familial separation: it also traces a gradual coming together of the two 'houses'. The members of the two households regularly come into contact with one another, meetings which Brontë uses to illustrate the differences between them. The example of Cathy and Heathcliff spying on the Lintons again serves to demonstrate this. The two houses are linked together further through the sequence of marriages in the text: those of Cathy and Edgar, of Heathcliff and Isabella, of Catherine and Linton and finally of Catherine and Hareton. The majority of these marriages, however, serve not to improve but to embitter the relations existing between them. Division rather than unity ironically emerges from most of the matrimonial unions. It is not until the final marriage of Catherine and Hareton at the very end of the novel, accompanied by the death of Heathcliff and his metaphorical 'wedding' in death with Cathy, that a true union of the two houses is effected.

Division within the individual is also a central aspect of the text. In exploring this issue, Brontë focuses upon the physical, mental and spiritual implications of division within her characters. Heathcliff and Cathy are clearly the most compelling examples of this in the novel, though many others, such as Hindley, Hareton, Catherine and Linton provide excellent cases. The presence of such division and its impact on the reader is suggested in the second chapter, when Lockwood, lying in his haunted bed, is faced with the three names: 'Catherine Earnshaw, here and there varied to Catherine Heathcliff, and then again to Catherine Linton.' Like the confused Lockwood, the reader is baffled by the confusion of identity both within and between characters, multiplied by the generational repetition of names. This proliferation of names, however, also illustrates the extent to which internal division occurs in the characters Brontë draws.

Cathy and Heathcliff are excellent examples of such internal division. Their relationship incorporates intimacy and distance, acceptance and rejection, care and recklessness, passion and coldness simultaneously. Division takes on a symbolic power, demonstrating their need for each other at the same time as it makes obvious the impossibility of their earthly union. Theirs is a love so powerful that its fulfilment is impossible. So close are they to one another that Cathy even goes to the extreme of claiming 'I am Heathcliff'.

Where such a spiritual affinity exists, the onset of conflict and division are perhaps an inevitability. Following her stay at the Lintons, Cathy returns like a young lady — she has already taken a step away from the 'ungentlemanly', racially and socially suspect Heathcliff and has moved towards the world of Edgar, thus establishing the central and most divisive triangle of the novel, a situation finally cemented by the marriage of Cathy and Edgar. From this point on, the endurance of the physical, mental and spiritual symptoms of division becomes a strange necessity to Cathy and Heathcliff and leads them into ever more extreme manifestations of their love/hate for each other. Their evident need to gratify these desires by tormenting each other embodies the power of the division and the passion they feel. This passion is evident whenever they meet, but is perhaps most devastatingly displayed shortly before Cathy's death in childbirth, when Heathcliff comes to visit her. Nelly Dean, who witnesses their meeting, is shocked, as is the reader, by the brutal and extremely physical manifestation of their emotions, more like the meeting of animals than of humans. It is evident that such feelings could never be contained within an earthly marriage. So strong are their emotions that they can only be consummated in the 'marriage' of their souls in death, where they achieve complete unity both within themselves and with each other.

Division, then, is a concept deeply engrained within Wuthering Heights. On individual, familial and societal levels, it is seen to exist and to exert a powerful influence, and the reader is forever aware of its existence as a driving force. It is, therefore, wholly appropriate that as the novel opened with division, so it should end with an image of division. Transported to the lonely churchyard at Gimmerton, the reader observes the tombs of Cathy, Heathcliff and Edgar. Even united in the state of death, Brontë is at pains to identify the differences between them: Edgar, the most conventional of the three, lies entirely within the consecrated ground; Cathy, symbolically between Edgar and Heathcliff, is half in and half out of the churchyard, semi-sanctified; Heathcliff is buried entirely outside the confines of holy ground. Their division persists even in death. The holy 'half' of Cathy remains within the churchyard to rest with her lawful husband, Edgar, while her unholy 'half' runs wild on the moors with her soul's completion, Heathcliff.

Using the critics

The role of literary criticism and literary theory in the study of literature at both AS and A2 is central. Assessment Objective 4 requires students specifically to 'articulate informed, independent judgements, showing understanding of different interpretations of literary texts by different readers'.

While this does not necessarily mean that all such interpretations should be by established literary critics or propound particular theoretical readings, the implication that these should be covered as part of advanced study is clear, especially where incisive and detailed analysis is required. Furthermore, the emphasis placed on a range of readings makes the use of criticism essential to success.

The following is an extract from the AQA specification, developing some of the implications of Assessment Objective 4:

Candidates will be expected to show awareness of the following:

- that, as readers, we are influenced by our own experiences, actual or imagined, and that our cultural background has an effect on our interpretation; thus the interpretation of literary texts, or the determination of their significance, can depend on the interpretative stance taken by the reader
- that there might be significant differences in the way literary texts are understood in different periods, and by different individuals or social groups
- that texts do not reflect an external and objective reality; instead they embody attitudes and values
- that there are different ways of looking at texts, based on particular approaches and theories. Using these theories will require some understanding of critical concepts and terminology
- that literary texts are frequently open-ended, so ambiguity and uncertainty are central to the reading of texts. Examination tasks will therefore expect candidates to take part in genuine critical enquiry rather than responding to tasks where the teacher/examiner already knows the 'right' answer.

Pages 75–80 of this guide offer a wide selection of critical extracts, looking in detail at a range of issues innate within the study of the Gothic. Pages 80–83 are relevant too, offering a more extended and applied analysis of readings of *Wuthering Heights* from Marxist, Freudian and feminist critical standpoints.

You need to think carefully about how critical material should be used. The emphasis in examination specifications is placed firmly upon a student's ability to recognise and evaluate the validity of interpretations from a multiplicity of viewpoints. Approaching a text from a single critical perspective, therefore, or prioritising one at the expense of others is neither desirable nor helpful. Successful students apply and develop their critical thinking about the set text in the light of a variety of secondary critical texts.

It is essential, however, that you do not see the use of critical quotation as a virtue in its own right. Unthinking application of critical material is at best redundant and at worst prevents students from thinking for themselves. The key to successful application of literary criticism and literary theory is to use it as a basis for argument. There are three basic positions that can be adopted:

(1) To agree with a critical proposition and to use this to support an argument or part of an argument.
(2) To agree with qualifications with a proposition; identify clearly what are the areas of agreement, but go on to develop areas of disagreement, qualification, modification or extension of the ideas.
(3) To disagree with a proposition, explaining why.

All of these stances can be developed by going on to propose alternative critical or theoretical possibilities and evaluating the validity of one critical perspective over another in relation to the text or passage under consideration. To extend and enrich a response, the criticism used must be engaged with. Students need to identify clearly the issues raised by the critic, apply these in detail to the set text — which must always remain the primary focus of the response — and then evaluate by giving a personal judgement.

Further study

Wide reading is an essential ingredient in the success of the best candidates. A carefully selected reading of other texts by the authors you are studying, critical works relating to the set text and other texts written within the same genre is invaluable in helping you to understand the context of the text you are working on for examination. As you read, note features shared between the texts, explaining how this enlightens your reading of the set text.

The following list is intended to give a range of reading material for the Gothic genre. Not all are conventionally established Gothic texts; they do, however, draw upon the conventions of Gothic to a significant extent, or play with the reader's knowledge of Gothic conventions.

Fiction

Ackroyd, P. *Hawksmoor* (1986).
Austen, J. *Northanger Abbey* (1818).
Carter, A. *The Magic Toyshop* (1967).
Collins, W. *Basil* (1852), *No Name* (1852), *The Woman in White* (1860).
Conan Doyle, Sir A. *The Hound of the Baskervilles* (1901), *Tales of Twilight and the Unseen* (1922).
Dacre, C. *Zofloya, or The Moor* (1806).

le Fanu, S. *Uncle Silas* (1864), *The Wyvern Mystery* (1869).

Gaskell, E. *Gothic Tales* (first published as a collection in 2000).

Godwin, W. *Caleb Williams, or Things as They Are* (1794).

Hawthorne, N. *The Scarlet Letter* (1850).

Hill, S. *The Woman in Black* (1983), *The Mist in the Mirror* (1992).

James, H. *The Aspern Papers* (1888), *The Turn of the Screw* (1898).

James, M. R. *Casting the Runes and Other Stories* (1931).

Lee, S. *The Recess, or A Tale of Other Times* (1785).

Lewis, M. *The Monk* (1796).

Machen, A. *The Great God Pan* (1913).

Maturin, C. *Melmoth the Wanderer* (1820).

Murdoch, I. *The Unicorn* (1963).

Peake, M. *The Gormenghast Trilogy* (1946–59).

Poe, E. A. *The Fall of the House of Usher* (1839), *The Black Cat* (1842), *The Pit and the Pendulum* (1842).

Radcliffe, A. *The Romance of the Forest* (1792), *The Mysteries of Udolpho* (1794), *The Italian* (1797).

Reeve, C. *The Old English Baron* (1778).

Shelley, M. *Frankenstein* (1818), *Valperga* (1823), *The Last Man* (1826), *Lodore* (1835), *Rambles in Germany and Italy* (1844).

Stoker, B. *Dracula* (1897).

Walpole, H. *The Castle of Otranto* (1764).

Wells, H. G. *The Island of Dr Moreau* (1896).

Wilde, O. *The Picture of Dorian Gray* (1891).

Poetry

William Blake, *The Four Zoas* (1893).

Lord Byron, *The Giaour* (1813).

S. T. Coleridge, *The Rime of the Ancient Mariner* (1798).

John Keats, *La Belle Dame sans Merci* (1819).

Edgar Allan Poe, *The Raven* (1845).

Edward Young, *The Complaint, or, Night-thoughts on Life, Death and Immortality* (1742).

Criticism

Bloom, C. (ed.) (1998) *Gothic Horror: A Reader's Guide from Poe to King and Beyond*, Macmillan.

Davenport-Hines, R. (1998) *Gothic: Four Hundred Years of Excess, Horror, Evil and Ruin*, Fourth Estate.

Gilbert, S. and Gubar, S. (1979) *The Madwoman in the Attic: The Woman Writer and the Nineteenth-Century Literary Imagination*, Yale University Press.

Haggerty, G. (1989) *Gothic Fiction/Gothic Form*, Pennsylvania State University Press.

Kilgour, M. (1995) *The Rise of the Gothic Novel*, Routledge.

Punter, D. (1996) *The Literature of Terror*, Longman.

Stevens, D. (2000) *The Gothic Tradition*, Cambridge University Press.